Access *for*

WINDOWS 95

FOR BUSY PEOPLE

Access for
WINDOWS 95
FOR BUSY PEOPLE

Alan R. Neibauer

Osborne/**McGraw-Hill**

Berkeley / New York / St. Louis / San Francisco / Auckland / Bogotá
Hamburg / London / Madrid / Mexico City / Milan / Montreal / New Delhi
Panama City / Paris / São Paulo / Singapore / Sydney / Tokyo / Toronto

Osborne/**McGraw-Hill**
2600 Tenth Street
Berkeley, California 94710
U.S.A.

For information on translations or book distributors outside the U.S.A., or to arrange bulk purchase discounts for sales promotions, premiums, or fundraisers, please contact Osborne/**McGraw-Hill** at the above address.

Access for Windows 95 For Busy People

1234567890 DOC 99876

ISBN 0-07-882112-6

Acquisitions Editor: Joanne Cuthbertson
Project Editor: Mark Karmendy
Copy Editor: Kathryn Hashimoto
Proofreader: Stefany Otis
Indexer: Matthew Spence
Graphic Artist: Marla J. Shelasky
Computer Designers: Roberta Steele, Leslee Bassin
Quality Control Specialist: Joe Scuderi
Series and Cover Designer: Ted Mader Associates
Series Illustration: Daniel Barbeau

To my bride of 30 years

About the Author

Alan Neibauer has published over 20 popular books on computer hardware and software since 1985, including *Word for Windows 95 Made Easy*. A graduate of the Wharton School, University of Pennsylvania, Neibauer has spent 14 years teaching computer science at the high school, college, and corporate levels, and is a popular corporate trainer on Microsoft Access. When not writing about computers, he practices Tai Kwon Do by the New Jersey shoreline.

Contents
at a glance

Contents

Part 2

ACKNOWLEDGMENTS

Every new writing project starts with a fresh burst of enthusiasm, but all too often the excitement quickly dies down. When Joanne Cuthbertson first approached me to write this book, I tended to attribute her ebullience to her consummate professionalism—that blend of editor, cheerleader, and salesperson that marks a successful acquisitions editor. However, after seeing the concept and design for the book, and the work of fellow series authors Christian Crumlish and Ron Mansfield, I was totally enamored.

The combination of Dan Barbeau's characters and Ted Mader's sophisticated design sets the perfect tone. Here is truly a series for those of us who need to learn, but are too busy with the necessities of life to waste any time.

It was also evident that the enthusiasm wasn't isolated to just a few of us—it spilled over to everyone at Osborne who worked on this series. My thanks to project editor Mark Karmendy, copyeditor Kathryn Hashimoto, and acquisitions assistant Heidi Poulin, for keeping up the momentum and excitement. Thanks also to the Osborne production team: Marla J. Shelasky, Leslee Bassin, Roberta Steele, Lance Ravella, Peter F. Hancik, Richard Whitaker, and Joe Scuderi—all of whom worked very hard on a tight project. Special thanks to technical editor Leigh Yafa. It wasn't easy for Leigh to work from beta to beta, trying to look backward and forward at the same time.

I also want to thank Microsoft's beta support team, particularly Susan Fetter, Melissa Frix, and Roger Harui, and the hundreds of beta testers who shared their ideas and knowledge over the CompuServe forum.

Finally, thanks to Barbara, my wife and best friend. Somehow she maintains her smile and sense of humor in spite of having me around the house.

INTRODUCTION

Finding just the right book for your needs is not always easy, especially facing the hundreds of competing titles in the book store. Suppose you're looking for a book on Access, which isn't much of a stretch since you're reading this now. What goes through your mind? If you are busy, like most of us, you might be thinking, "How much time can I really afford learning this program?" After all, you have Access so you can start really using it, not just reading about it.

A lot of books, unfortunately, are written to impress or entertain you. That's not necessarily a bad thing if you're cuddling by the fire with a spine-tingling thriller, or feeding your brain cells with Umberto Eco's latest foray into antiquity. No one buys a computer book for its literary value. A computer book has one purpose, and one purpose only—to get you productive as quickly and as painlessly as possible. It should be easy to read, pleasing to the eye, but right to the point.

To make my point, that's why we've published the Busy People series. It is expressly for people who want to get a job done, and who don't have any time to waste; people who want to know how to get something done, in as little time as possible, but who won't be satisfied with sketchy information and half-hearted examples.

I KNOW YOU'RE IN A HURRY, SO...

Enough of the required introduction. If you haven't yet installed Access onto your computer, jump right ahead to Appendix A where you'll learn how to do so quickly and painlessly. If someone has set up Access for you already, just remember that the appendix is there—you'll need to refer to it if you have to add parts of Access to set up features that were not installed, or remove features to clear extra space in your disk drive.

In Appendix B you'll find an excellent introduction to Windows 95, written with loving care by my fellow author Christian Crumlish (whose book *Word for Windows 95 for Busy People,* by the way, is one great way to learn Microsoft Word).

When you've got Access installed, and you know your way somewhat around Windows 95, then you're ready to start. Because you are busy, I suggest starting at the beginning. In the first chapter of this book you'll learn how to create databases—and pretty sophisticated ones at that—in less time than the average coffee break. I call these Almost Instant Databases. The next several chapters show you how to use these databases, so you can enter, edit, and sort information, select specific information when you need it, and print forms and reports. If you are busy, these Almost Instant Databases can satisfy most of your database needs, and make you a hero or heroine around the office.

HOW ACCESS FOR WINDOWS 95 DIFFERS FROM EARLIER VERSIONS

Access is more than just a rehash of its previous versions. Certainly is takes full advantage of Windows 95 features such as long file names, shortcut menus, and a super new help system, but it has been loaded with new and improved features as well. It's now easy to create complete relational databases with Database Wizard, and even fine-tune your work with the Table Analyzer Wizard and Performance Analyzer. Lookup Wizard lets you create a list to look up values in other tables, and Simple Query Wizard lets you create some rather sophisti- cated queries—*Simple* refers to how easy it is to use, not necessary the type of queries it can create.

There are new form and report wizards, and you can automatically format an entire form and copy styles from one object to another. There is even the User-Level Security Wizard that secures and encrypts a database, then lets you grant permissions to users and groups of your choosing.

Microsoft has added scores of features to make Access more powerful but easier to use. If you've never used Access before, you'll be impressed by its ease of use and by its capabilities. If you're familiar with previous versions, you'll just love what they've done for you.

THINGS YOU MIGHT WANT TO KNOW ABOUT THIS BOOK

Like Access, this book is designed to make your life easier. You can go through it chapter by chapter, creating your own databases, forms, and reports using our examples as a guide. You can also use this book as a reference. Trying to do something right now? Just go directly to the section in the book, find out how to do it, and then just do it. We've even added the following special elements to make sure you don't waste any time.

Fast Forwards

Each chapter begins with a section called *FAST FORWARD*. FAST FORWARDS are step-by-step directions, with illustrations, that quickly guide you through the tasks explained in the chapter. Sometimes that's all you'll need to read to perform an Access function. But if you need more, you'll find page references so you can just flip to the section in the chapter that discusses the subject in detail.

Habits & Strategies

As you're reading, look for *habits & strategies*. These offer timesaving tips, and some gentle pushes so you learn good Access work habits from the get go. Once you learn bad habits it's often difficult to find your way back, so we've added these to keep you on the straight and narrow.

Shortcuts

SHORTCUTS are our special gift to the busy person. When we found a faster way to do something you'll see a note in the margin, identified by a businessman leaping the fence in a single bound. The shortcut might not be as complete as the detailed instructions in the chapter, but it gets the job done.

Cautions

Access is a pretty well-behaved program, but it is still possible to mess up. If there's a possibility that you can find a way to waste valuable time, we'll warn you ahead of time. When you see a CAUTION on a page, read it first. You'll find them worthwhile.

Definitions

Because you're busy, we don't want to waste your time with a lot of computer mumbo-jumbo, and we explain everything we can in plain words. But when there are terms that are not in the common vernacular, or take on a different meaning in Access, look for this body-builder in the margin.

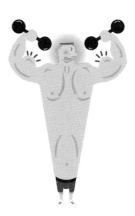

Step By Step

There are Access tasks that are best explained by just a series of simple steps. Look for these blue *step by step* boxes to walk you through the steps. The illustrations from the program will show you want to look for on your screen.

Throughout the book, cross-references and other minor asides appear in the margins.

Upgrade Notes

If you've used an early version of Access, then keep an eye out for *upgrade notes*. These will report new or improved features, or a new way of doing something.

SO WHAT'S NEXT?

The world of Access awaits. Jump right in there and build that database. If you get frustrated, or just want to share a thought or so about Access in your spare time, I'm standing by at 70365770@compuserve.com.

Part 1

JUST THE FACTS

Almost Instant Databases

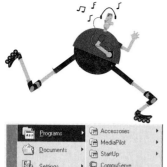

FAST FORWARD

START ACCESS ➤ *pp 6-8*
1. Click on the Start button in the taskbar.
2. Point to Programs.
3. Click on Microsoft Access.

Asset Tracking   Book Collection   Contact Management

CREATE A DATABASE ➤ *pp 8-11, 18-22*
1. Start Access.
2. Click on Database Wizard.
3. Click on OK.
4. Double-click on template.
5. Enter database name and click on Create.
6. Click on Finish.

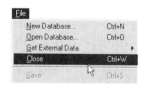

DISPLAY PARTS OF THE DATABASE ➤ *pp 11-15*
To see a database object, click on its tab:
- Tables
- Queries
- Forms
- Reports
- Macros
- Modules

CLOSE A DATABASE ➤ *p 22*
- Select Close from the File menu.
- Or, click on the Close box in the Access title bar.

OPEN A DATABASE ➤ *pp 22-24*
- When starting Access, double-click on the database in the Startup dialog box.
- When Access is already open, click on the Open Database button, and double-click on the database in the Open dialog box.

Wizard: *A series of dialog boxes that guide you through the process of a complete task.*

Database: *A repository of information.*

Table: *A collection of information relating to a specific category of information.*

Unless you're a control freak, you don't have to design every database from the ground up. To get you up and running quickly, this chapter introduces you to the Database Wizard, a nifty tool that lets you create a complete, sophisticated database with a few clicks of the mouse. You get a complete database—even with sample information if you want it. It may not have every feature that you'll need, but you'll learn you can easily add tables, forms, reports, and other elements later on. The idea is that the Wizard will let you create and start using a database—for all of that important work you have to do—in a short time. Then as you become more familiar with Access, you modify and expand the database to perform all of the functions you need.

ANATOMY OF A DATABASE

Before we dive in, though, let's review a few important concepts and terms. There aren't that many of them, but it's important to spend a few minutes getting oriented. Let's start with the term *database*.

A database is a place where you store information. You can consider a box of three-by-five-inch index cards to be a database. You can also consider a filing cabinet full of folders and papers to be a database. In fact, let's do that. Picture a database as a large filing cabinet holding all of your company's records. Put all of those records on a computer, have a program that finds, edits, and prints information, and you have a database. Simple.

Now look at the labels on the filing cabinet drawers. One label might tell you that the drawer contains employee records, while another drawer contains client information, another contains invoices, and another contains inventory. In database-speak we call each of these drawers a *table*.

definitions

Record: *A collection of information about one object in the table.*

Field: *A specific category of information in each record.*

For example, the Clients table contains the information you need about your clients. The Invoice table contains information about invoices. The tables are separate, but do they have anything in common? Sure. They all contain information about your company, so they are all in the same database.

Now open a cabinet drawer. In the invoice drawer, you'll see a series of invoices. Each invoice contains information about one order. This is what database geeks call a *record*. What does each record in the client drawer contain? The name, address, and other information about a client.

OK, now look at a sheet of paper containing that client's information. Each piece of information—such as the name or phone number—is called a *field*. And finally, each field is simply made up of individual letters, numbers, or punctuation marks.

So let's review the parts of a database by working backwards—from the smallest entity to the largest.

- Individual characters make up a *field*—a single piece of information.
- The fields are categories of information, collected in *records*—the information about one client, invoice, or whatever.
- The records are contained in *tables*, which store all of the information about clients, invoices, or whatever.
- Tables are contained in *databases*.
- Databases are stored on your disk.

STARTING ACCESS

Before you can start Access, you need to start your computer and Windows 95. Once Windows 95 is running, start Access as follows:

1. Click on the Start button in the taskbar.
2. Point to Programs—you only have to point to it, there's no need to click!
3. Click on Microsoft Access.

If Access is not listed on the Programs menu, then either one of two things has occurred. Either you did not yet install Access on your system, or Access is contained in a group within the Programs option. Look for a listing such as MSOffice or Office95. Point to it and see if

Access is there. If it is, click on it. Otherwise, you'll have to install Access; gather together your Access disks or CD, and follow the setup instructions in Appendix A. Then come back, please.

After Access starts, you'll see the dialog box shown in Figure 1.1. Since everything must have a name in Windows, this box is officially called the Startup dialog box. You can create a new blank database or use the Database Wizard. (If you already created a database, you'll be able to open it from this dialog box, as well.) If you create a blank database, you'll have to create the tables, forms, and reports yourself. It's not difficult; it just takes more time than letting Access do it for you.

Behind the Startup dialog box is the Access screen, which is shown in Figure 1.2 without the dialog box blocking your view. At the top of the screen is the title bar, menu bar, and toolbar. The menu bar contains options for performing Access functions. The toolbar contains buttons for performing the most typical Access functions. To use the toolbar, just point to the button for the function you want to perform and click. If you're not sure what function a button performs, don't worry. When you point to a button, Access displays a ToolTip—a small box showing the button's name—and you can read a description of the button at the bottom of the screen. The buttons in the toolbar will change depending on what you are doing in Access, and some of the buttons may be dimmed. You'll learn how to use the toolbar throughout this book, but take a look at it now so you can see how it changes.

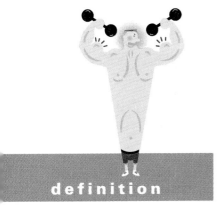

definition

Dimmed: *The appearance of a toolbar button, menu option, or dialog box option in a light shade of gray, indicating that it cannot be selected.*

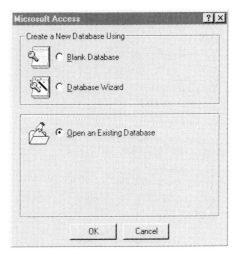

Figure 1.1 The Startup dialog box appears whenever you start Access—use it to create a new database or open an existing one

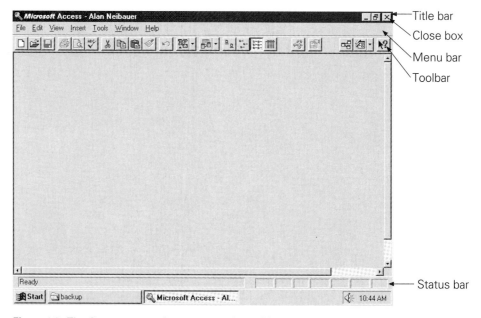

Title bar
Close box
Menu bar
Toolbar
Status bar

Figure 1.2 The Access screen is your control panel for working with and creating databases

At the bottom of the screen is the status bar. Here Access tells you something about the state of your system. On the left of the status bar, for example, it will report the current view—the type of function you are performing—or the function of the toolbar button you are pointing to with the mouse. On the right are status boxes, showing if your CAPS LOCK, NUM LOCK, or SCROLL LOCK keys are on, or if you are inserting or overtyping (replacing) characters as you type. Between the toolbar and the status bar are your database and its various parts.

CREATING AN ALMOST INSTANT DATABASE

To see how easy it is to create a database, let's create a database right now. We'll create a database to track employee expenses (which will please your accountant, the IRS, and your bottom line). The database will have four related tables, and it will be complete with seven forms and three reports. There will even be a menu that lets you perform the most typical functions. And all of this with just a few clicks. No more theory and technobabble—let's just jump right in.

habits & strategies

When you need to create a database, try the Database Wizard first—it can save you a lot of time.

If you do not see a database that seems perfect for your needs, look for one that comes close. You can then modify it to suit your needs.

Let's start the Database Wizard and create the database. The Startup dialog box should be on your screen, so let's go.

1. Click on the Database Wizard option button. This tells Access that you want it to create a database for you.
2. Click on OK. The New dialog box will appear with two pages, General and Database. You use the General page to start a blank database, which would require you to design the tables yourself.
3. Click on the Databases tab to see the page shown in Figure 1.3. In this dialog box, you select one of the existing database types. They include many of the common database functions that users need.
4. Point to Expenses and double-click. The File New Database box appears. In this box, you give the database a name and you tell Access where on your disk you want to save it. By default, Access saves databases in the My Documents directory. Access will give it a name based on the type, such as Friends1 or Contact Management1.

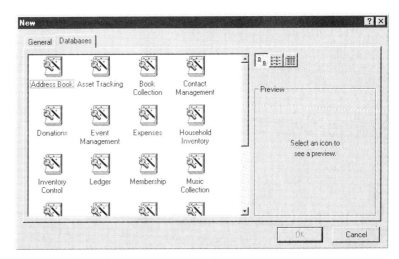

Figure 1.3 New dialog box to select database type

9

Default: *This happens when you don't change a thing and just go with the flow. You'll see this word a lot in any book about computer software.*

Switchboard: *A special form that lets you perform specific options like a menu.*

5. Type **Office Expenses** and then click on Create.

6. Access does a few chores, and after a few moments the first Wizard dialog box appears as in Figure 1.4. This box shows you the type of information that the database will store. At the bottom of the Wizard dialog box are four buttons: Cancel, Back, Next, and Finish.

   - Click on Cancel to stop the Wizard.
   - Click on Back to go to the previous Wizard dialog box.
   - Click on Next to move to the next dialog box.
   - Click on Finish to complete the Wizard using the default values for the remaining dialog box.

7. Click on Finish—you're done. Access now creates your database.

Depending on your computer, the time to create a database can take several minutes or longer, so be patient. First, you'll see a blank database window on the screen (you'll learn more about this later), and then Access creates the tables, forms, reports, and other elements that make up the database. When the database is created, the Switchboard form will appear, as shown in Figure 1.5.

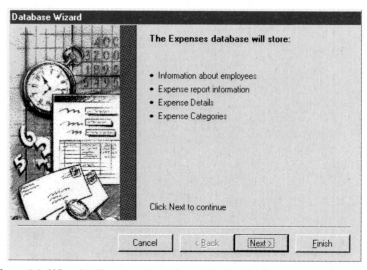

Figure 1.4 Wizard telling you what information the database stores

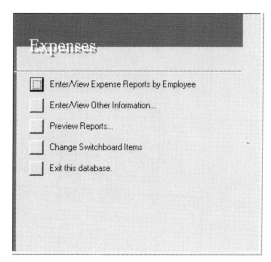

Figure 1.5 Switchboard form

A QUICK TOUR OF THE ALMOST INSTANT DATABASE

There are quite a few parts to an Access database, so let's take a minute to orient ourselves to this new terrain.

What you're looking at now is the Switchboard. Access provides switchboards for the databases it creates with the Wizard, but they will not automatically appear in databases you create yourself. Switchboards are a great feature that let you work with an Almost Instant Database, so you should get to know them. In front of each item in the Switchboard is an icon, like this:

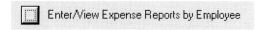

To perform the function listed, click on the icon.

Access Forms

Click on the icon next to Enter/View Expense Reports by Employee, the first option on the Switchboard. Access displays a form, as shown in Figure 1.6.

Forms are a great way to work with a database. Not only can you use them to enter, edit, and review information, but you can also print

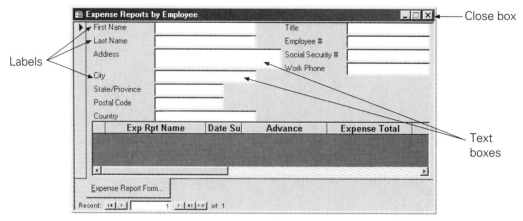

Figure 1.6 The Employee form in an Almost Instant Database

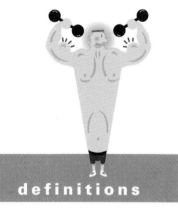

Form: *An electronic version of a paper form that you use to enter information into the database, to change the information, and to view it on the screen.*

Report: *Used for printing information from the database, performing calculations, and summarizing large amounts of data.*

copies of the forms for reference. In most cases, the fields in a form correspond to the fields in an underlying table. However, you can also have calculated fields—categories of information calculated from the values in other fields. Calculated fields are not part of any table; they just appear on the form.

The form contains labels and text boxes. The labels show the field name so you know what to type in the text box. Because there is no data in the table yet, the form is blank. This is actually a special type of form that is two forms in one. On the top will be information about an employee, and on the bottom will be a list of that employee's expenses. The form gets its information from two different tables. Notice that when this form is displayed, fewer buttons in the toolbar are dimmed. This means that you use more of the buttons—perform more functions—than when the Switchboard form was on the screen.

Now click on the form's Close box to return to the Switchboard.

Access Reports

You can print forms, but they are primarily designed to be used onscreen. When you want hardcopy, use a report.

To see a report, click on Preview Reports, the third item on the Switchboard. A new Switchboard menu appears with three options—two types of reports that you can print, and the option to return to the main Switchboard. Remember, when an instruction in this book says to click on a Switchboard item, click on the icon next to it.

Click on the first option—Preview the Expense Report Summary by Category. A box appears asking for the starting and ending dates—so you can print expenses that occurred between two dates. Since there's no information in this database, you won't be able to preview the report, so click on the close box to return to the switchboard. Figure 1.7, however, shows how the report would appear with information—notice the different toolbar. Click on the Close box to return to the Switchboard, and then click on Return to Main Switchboard.

The Database Window

Forms, reports, and other objects are parts of the database. You can access some of the parts through the Switchboard, but you can access all of the parts from the *database window*, the main interface to an Access database. Let's look at the database window now.

So far, you've closed one window before opening another. This time, click on the Database Window button—the third button from the right in the toolbar. Access opens the main database window, as shown in Figure 1.8, moving the Switchboard into the background. No matter what type of window you have open in Access, you can always click on the Database Window button to see the main database window. Switch between open windows using the Window menu.

Because of the way Microsoft designed the Almost Instant Databases, some items in switchboards, forms, and reports may not appear formatted correctly or shown in their entirety.

If you are new to Windows, read Appendix B in this book to learn how to work with Windows applications.

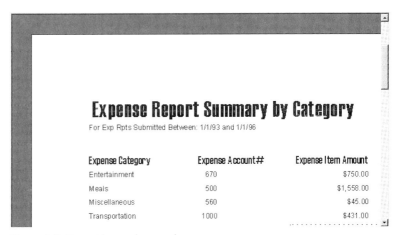

Expense Report Summary by Category
For Exp Rpts Submitted Between: 1/1/93 and 1/1/96

Expense Category	Expense Account #	Expense Item Amount
Entertainment	670	$750.00
Meals	500	$1,558.00
Miscellaneous	560	$45.00
Transportation	1000	$431.00

Figure 1.7 Report in preview mode

If you close the Switchboard by mistake, the database window appears minimized at the bottom of the Access screen. Click on the Restore button to display the database window.

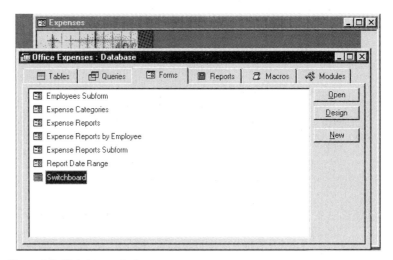

Figure 1.8 Database window

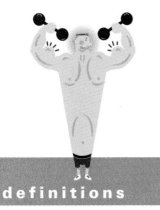

definitions

Object: *A fancy way of saying "things," and an attempt to confuse those of us who are not computer scientists.*

Datasheet: *The display of table information in rows and columns. The column headings are the field names, and each row is another record.*

The database window represents the open database. On top of the database window are tabs that you use to move from page to page by selecting Tables, Queries, Forms, Reports, Macros, and Modules. For example, to see a list of tables in the database, click on the Tables tab. To see a list of forms, click on the Forms tab. Now click on each of the tabs to see what objects have been created for this sample table.

On the right of the database window are three command buttons:

- *Open* displays the table, form, or query selected in the database window. The button is replaced by the Preview button when viewing the Reports page, and by Run when viewing the Macros and Modules pages.
- *Design* lets you modify the table, form, report, or query selected in the database window.
- *New* lets you create a new table, form, report, or query.

Datasheets

Forms and reports are two ways that you can look at the information in a table. When you use a form, you see one or more records at a time, depending on the form's design. When you want to see as many records as can fit on your screen at one time, look at the table as a datasheet.

The Switchboard items table is a special table that stores the options shown in the Switchboards. You can add items to this table to add items to the Switchboard form.

In the database window, you can double-click on a table, form, or query to open it. Likewise, you can double-click on a report to preview it, or on a macro or module to run it.

You access datasheets from the Tables page of the database window, so let's look at a datasheet now. Click on the Tables tab to see the list of tables.

Click on Employees in the list of tables, and then click on Open.

The table appears like a spreadsheet—a series of rows and columns—as shown in Figure 1.9. There's no data in this table, so there's only one blank row under the field names. The notation (Auto-Number) means that Access will automatically number the records as you enter them, inserting the number in the Employee ID field.

Figure 1.9 Table in Datasheet view

Select Close from the File menu to close the datasheet and return to the database window.

Other Parts of a Database

All Almost Instant Databases come complete with forms, reports, and datasheets. They won't have any queries, macros, and modules, which are the other three parts that can make up a database—you have to create them yourself.

A *query* is a question you ask to find information in the table. "Who hasn't paid their bill in over 30 days?" is a query (and an important one if you plan on staying in business). What the question really tells Access is "show me the records of clients who have unpaid invoices dated over 30 days ago." Each time you ask the question, you may get a different answer—depending on the status of your receivables at the time. When you save the query in Access, you are saving the question, not the answer. You can then run the query to get the latest information.

A *macro* lets you perform a series of Access tasks by issuing just one command. A *module* is similar, but it is much more complicated and requires some computer programming knowledge. Macros and modules are for advanced users.

Learning About Relationships

Most of the time, you don't want to put all of your information in one table. It's like the old adage about putting all of your eggs in one basket. For one reason, the more fields and information you put in a table, the more difficult it is to work with. Sometimes, you divide the information into more than one table, and then relate the tables together.

For example, suppose you're still using paper forms to record your company's information. If you have more information than can fit on one page, you use a second or third sheet of paper to complete a form. So while one piece of paper contains address information on client X, another piece of paper contains credit information. When you want to look at address information, you just need the first page. When you want credit information you just need the second. The two pages are related, however, because they both discuss client X. How do you know? You look at the top of both pages and you make sure they both have the same client name, client number, or some other piece of information that links the two together.

The same principle applies to your computer database. You divide the information into more than one table. You then relate the tables to each other, using one or more fields to match the records in one table with the records in the other.

In a database, you can create several types of relationships. In what's called a one-to-one relationship—a true monogamy—every record in one table is related to just one record in the other table. So for each client address record, there is just one client credit record.

You can also have a polygamous relationship, called one-to-many. This means that a record in one table can be related to one *or more* records in another table. For example, you certainly hope that each client places more than one order. So a client record, in the client table, can be related to more than one record in the order table. How does the database keep track? Because the client name or number in the client record matches the client name or number in the order record. Note that the one-to-many relationship works only in one direction. An order can only be from one client, so each order in the order table is connected to only one client record.

Information is often divided into several tables, not because of space problems, but because it makes it easier and more efficient to process.

CAUTION

There is also a relationship called many-to-many. Avoid it if you can!

Don't let the Relationships window throw you; it's really very easy to figure out. In fact, here we're just concerned with the overall meaning of the window, so if you don't feel you're ready to handle it, just skip ahead to the next section.

You can see how tables are related from the database window. Click on the Relationships button, which is the third button from the right when you're looking at the database window. Access opens the Relationships window, shown in Figure 1.10.

Each of the boxes in the window represents a table in the database. Within each box is a list of the table's fields. The line from one table to another shows what field is used to relate the tables, and the type of relationship. For example, there's a line from the EmployeeID field in the Employees table to the EmployeeID field in the Expense Reports table. The number 1, near the Employees table, shows that this is the "one" side of the relationship. The infinity symbol near the Expense Reports table indicates the "many" side—that each employee can have one or more expense report(s). If you looked at an expense report, you could tell which employee submitted it by looking at the EmployeeID.

There is also a one-to-many relationship between the Expense Reports table and the Expense Details table. The relation is connected by the ExpenseReportID field, which you can't see because the box is too small. In this case, the general information about the report is in the Expense Reports table, but the details explaining each expense is in the Expense Details table. The one-to-many relationship means that each expense report can include one or more expenses.

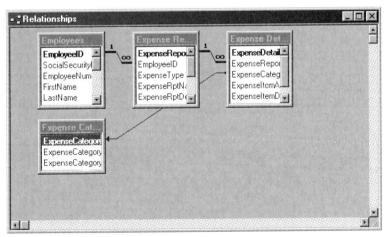

Figure 1.10 Relationships window showing how tables are related

Finally, there is a connection between the Expense Details table and the Expense Categories table. The relation is one-to-one, meaning that each Expense Details record is only about one expense category.

That's enough for now. Click on the Close box in the Relationships window to return to the database window.

CREATING A CUSTOM ALMOST INSTANT DATABASE

When you created the Office Expenses database, you clicked on Finish in the first Database Wizard dialog box. Access created the database using all of the default values. This means that it selects which fields to include in the tables and the style of forms and reports. If you don't feel comfortable being so passive, you can make other choices yourself by displaying additional Wizard dialog boxes.

Let's create another database now, this time working through each of the Database Wizard boxes, so you can see what choices you have in creating an Almost Instant Database.

1. Click on the New Database button in the toolbar, or select New Database from the File menu.
2. Click on the Database tab, and then double-click on Contact Management. The File New Database dialog box appears where you enter the database name.
3. Type **Contacts** and then click on Create. The first Wizard box appears listing the type of information that will be stored in this database.
4. Click on Next, instead of Finish, to display the next dialog box, shown in Figure 1.11.

The second Wizard box shows you the tables that are included with the database (on the left) and the fields that are included in the tables (on the right). You can also select from other optional fields that Access does not include by default, and you can select to have Access fill the database with sample data—not because you don't have enough contacts on your own, but so you can practice using the database with phony information.

Because the Contact information table is selected on the left, the fields in that table are shown on the right. The check mark next to the field name means that it will be included in the table.

Access will automatically close and save the open database when you create or open another.

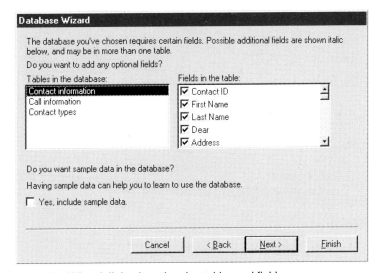

Figure 1.11   Wizard dialog box showing tables and fields

If you change your mind about the field, click on it again to remove the check mark. You can only remove the check mark from optional fields.

5. Scroll down the Fields in the Table list. Below the Work Extension field you'll see Home Phone. It is in italics and the check box is not checked. This means that it is an optional field—that you can have the Database Wizard include it if you want.

6. Click on the check box next to Home Phone to add it to the table, then continue scrolling the list to see other optional fields.

7. Click on the check box next to the Birthdate field.

8. Click on the Call Information and Contact Types tables to see their fields.

9. Click on Yes, include sample data. This way we can look at a table and form that actually has information in it.

10. Click on Next. This next Wizard dialog box, shown in Figure 1.12, lets you choose a design to use for the forms when you are working with the database. The names of the styles are on the right. When you click on a style, the panel on the left will illustrate its appearance. The word "Label" indicates how the name of the field will appear; the word "Data" indicates how the information that you type will appear.

11. Click on each of the types to see how they will appear.

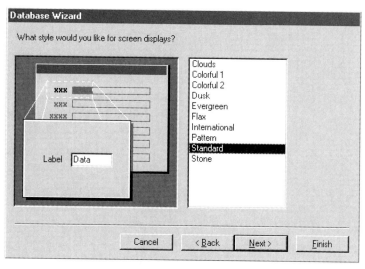

Figure 1.12 Wizard dialog box for form design

12. Click on Standard (the default setting) and then on Next. The next Wizard (Figure 1.13) shows the styles for printed reports. Click on each of the styles on the right to see how it appears on the left.

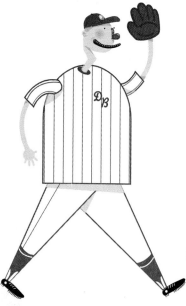

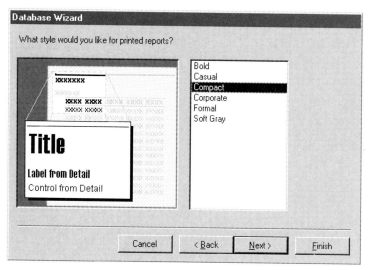

Figure 1.13 Wizard dialog box for report design

The Help option will show you how to work with the database. You have this book, so you don't need to select Help.

13. Click on Corporate and then on Next. This next dialog box (Figure 1.14) lets you enter the title for the database to use on the Switchboard, and asks if you want to include a picture on the main screen and in reports. If you select to include a picture, you'll need to find it using the Picture button, so leave this option alone for now.

14. The text in the box is selected, so type **Contacts** and then click on Next. The final dialog box has only two options. If you select Yes, start the database (the default option), Access will display the Switchboard when the Wizard ends.

15. Click on the Yes, start the database option to deselect it. This will prevent the Switchboard from displaying.

16. Click on Finish. After Access creates the database, it displays a message telling you so.

17. Click on OK to display the database window.

The database window looks the same as the one you saw previously—only the listed objects are different.

Click on the tabs to see the names of the tables, forms, and reports created as part of the database. Open one or two of the forms to see how they appear.

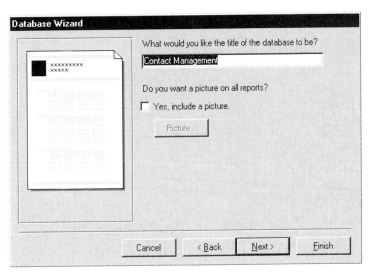

Figure 1.14 Wizard dialog box for title and picture

The Wizard Remembers

Once you select a look for forms and reports in the Database Wizard, the same styles will automatically be selected when you run the Wizard again. If you now create a database by selecting Finish in the first Wizard dialog box, for example, the new database will use the Corporate style for reports. To change the styles, you must select different options from the Wizard dialog box.

The Wizard does not remember if you've selected optional fields. The next time you create a database using the same template, the optional fields will not be selected by default.

OPENING A DATABASE

As you saw, Access closes the open database when you create another. In fact, you can't have more than one database open at a time. If you want to return to the previous database, you have to open it again.

You can open a database when you first start Access, or any time after. When you start Access, databases that you've created will be listed in the Startup dialog box, as shown in Figure 1.15. Double-click on the database name, or select it and then choose Open. To see databases that are not listed in the box, click on More Files.

To close a database yourself, choose Close from the File menu, or click on the Close box on the right side of the database window. You do not have to save it first—Access takes care of it or prompts you if any objects need to be saved.

Figure 1.15 Startup dialog box showing existing files

You can open Access and the database at the same time from the Windows 95 taskbar using the following steps.

OPENING A DATABASE step by step

1. Cick on the Start button.
2. Point to Documents.
3. Click on the database name.

Once you start Access, you can open a database using the File menu or the toolbar. Click on the File menu. At the bottom of the menu, you'll see the names of the last four databases that you worked on. To open one of the databases, just click on its name.

To open any database—even one not listed on the File menu—click on the Open Database button in the toolbar or select Open Database from the File menu to display the Open dialog box shown in Figure 1.16.

Windows 95 has new and improved Open and Save dialog boxes that Access and other applications use.

Now double-click on the name of the database you want to open (Office Expenses). Access opens the database and automatically displays the Switchboard form. Click on Exit this database to close the database.

You've done enough for one session. To exit Access, select Exit from the File menu, or click on the Close box on the right of the Access title bar. If you've made any changes to a database that were not saved, a dialog box will appear asking if you want to save the changes. This is Access's way of protecting you from your own mistakes.

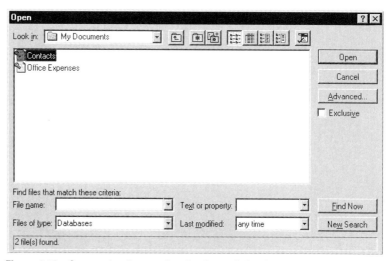

Figure 1.16 Open a database using the Open dialog box

SO WHAT'S NEXT?

You now know how to create a complete database, in as few as five clicks of the mouse. In Chapter 2, you'll learn how to use the Almost Instant Databases that you've created so you can start your own database projects.

CHAPTER 2

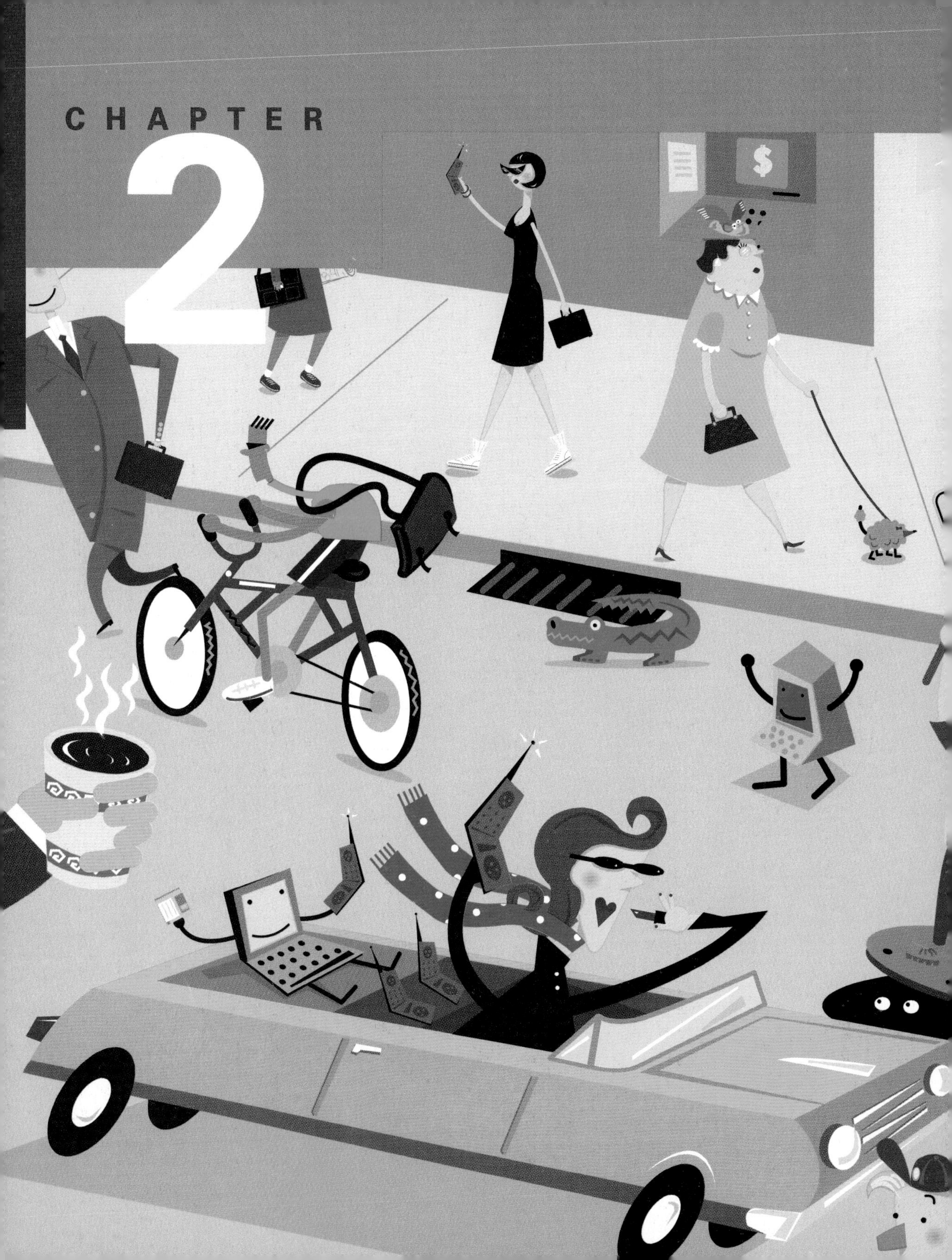

Using Forms—Almost Instant and Others

FAST FORWARD

NAVIGATE THROUGH FORMS ➤ *pp 30-31*
- Click First Record.
- Click Previous Record.
- Click in the Go to Record box (or press F5), type the record number, and press ENTER.
- Click on Next Record.
- Click on Last Record.

ADD A RECORD ➤ *p 31*
- Click on New Record.
- Or, press ENTER in last field of last record.

CANCEL CHANGES ➤ *p 36*
- Click Undo Current Field/Record to restore the current field or an entire record.

DELETE A RECORD ➤ *pp 36-37*
1. Display the record onscreen.
2. Click on the Delete Record button.

SORT RECORDS ➤ *pp 37-38*
1. Click in the field to use for the sort.
2. Click on Sort Ascending (left button) or Sort Descending (right button).

FILTER BY SELECTION ➤ *pp 39-40*
1. Click on the field containing the data to use for the filter.
2. Click on the Filter By Selection button.

FILTER BY EXCLUDING ➤ *p 40*

1. Right-click on the field containing the data to exclude from the filter.
2. Select Filter Excluding Selection.

FILTER BY FORM ➤ *p 40*

1. Click on the Filter By Form button.
2. Enter or select the field contents to use for the filter.
3. Click on OR and set OR operations.
4. Click on Apply Filter.

REMOVE A FILTER ➤ *p 42*

- Select Remove Filter/Sort from the Records menu.
- Or, click on the Remove Filter button.

Now that you've created your Almost Instant Database, it's about time you actually use it. There are three things that you'll want to do most often: add, find, and edit information. Your Almost Instant Databases let you work with information in either a datasheet or a form. Datasheets are useful because they display many records at a time. Because we're used to holding pieces of paper in our hands, however, forms more closely resemble the way we work with information in the real world. You can think of a form as a security blanket before graduating into the cold, hard world of databases—instead of changing your work habits to deal with information in a datasheet, start by working with something more familiar.

Don't skip this chapter, even if you don't plan on using Database Wizard forms. You can use the same techniques as explained in this chapter to change, sort, filter, and delete records in forms that you create yourself and in the Datasheet view as well.

A TOUR DE FORM

Start Access and open the Contacts database, as you learned in Chapter 1. Access will display the Switchboard. Click on Enter/View Other Informaion to see a second Switchboard. Click on the Enter/View Contact Types option to display the form shown in Figure 2.1.

Now look at the form in a little detail. The form contains labels and text boxes. The information in the text boxes represents the information in the table that's used for this form—in this case, a table named Contact Types, which is just coincidentally the same name as the form. If you change any information on the form or add new records using a form,

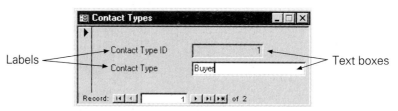

Figure 2.1 Contact Types form—lets you enter information easily and quickly

you are actually changing the contents of the table. So the form is more than just a pretty face. It is a way to work with the table in a nicely designed layout.

The insertion point (the blinking line) is in the Contact Type field. That's because you cannot enter or change the information in the Contact Type ID box. This is one of those AutoNumber fields that you saw in Chapter 1. Access will number the first record you enter as 1, the second record as 2, and so on.

On the left of the form is a selection bar (the vertical bar with a triangle at the top). If you want to select the entire form (for printing or copying, for example), you click on the selection bar. The triangle at the top of the bar shows that you are looking at the form, not entering or editing information in it.

At the bottom of the form are a series of buttons. You use these buttons to move from record to record:

In databases that don't have a switchboard, click on the Forms tab of the database window, and then double-click on the form you want to open.

Button	Name
⏮	First Record
◀	Previous Record
1	Go to Record
▶	Next Record
▶�	Last Record
▶✱	New Record

To use the Go to Record box, click in the box with the mouse or press F5, replace the number there with the record number you want to display, and then press ENTER.

The Previous Record button is dimmed, because there is no previous record—you're looking at the first one. Click on Next Record. The information in the form changes, and the form shows that you are looking at the second of two records.

Adding Records with a Form

You can add a new record by displaying a blank form and filling it out, just as you would do with paper forms. To add a new record, click on the New Record button. You can find the same button in two places—one in the toolbar, and the other next to the record navigation buttons; click on either one. Access dims the Next Record button,

When you click on Next Record when you're already at the end of the table, Access displays a blank form so you can insert a new record.

SHORTCUTS

Press CTRL-=(CTRL and the equal sign) or CTRL-+ (CTRL and the plus sign) to add a new record.

If you press ENTER after the last field and decide you do not want to insert another record, don't worry. Do not type anything on the form, and just go to another record or close the form. Access does not save blank forms with the table.

because there isn't a next record, and it dims the New Record button, because you're already in that mode.

The Contact Type ID field contains the AutoNumber indicator, and the insertion point is in the Contact Type field. Type **Friend**. As soon as you start typing, Access inserts the next ID number in the Contract Type ID field. Notice that it also replaces the triangle in the selection bar with the pencil icon, showing that you are making changes to the form. Now press ENTER. Because you were already in the last field, Access displays another blank form. Type **Relative** and then click on the New Record button to display another blank form. Now click on the Close box on the right side of the form's title bar to return to the Switchboard.

Pencil icon ⟶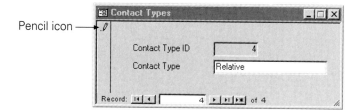

Working with Complex Forms

Not all forms are created equal. While the Contact Type form is pretty simple with just two fields, Almost Instant Database forms can be much more complex. As an example, click on the Return to Main Switchboard option, and then click on the Enter/View Contacts option to see the form shown in Figure 2.2. The information in the form represents the contents of the Contacts table. This is a more sophisticated form that contains buttons at the bottom. The buttons run macros. For example, clicking on Calls will show a list of phone calls. Clicking on Dial will dial your phone. Clicking on 1 or 2 changes pages of this two-page form.

This form contains a number of text boxes, divided into two pages. Before adding a new record to the table, practice moving around the form. At this point, you are viewing the form, not changing it. The contents of the current field is highlighted, or it appears in reverse video. To move forward from field to field, press TAB, ENTER, or the RIGHT ARROW or DOWN ARROW keys. Move backward by pressing SHIFT-TAB, or the LEFT ARROW or UP ARROW keys. Press HOME to move to the first text box, and press END to move to the last text box. You can also click on a text box.

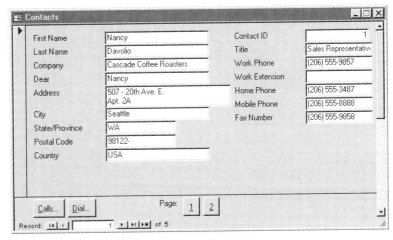

Figure 2.2 More sophisticated Contacts forms

If you selected a style other than Standard5 when you ran the Database Wizard, clicking on the Page 2 button may not display the entire second page of the form. If this occurs, use the scroll bar to scroll the entire second page into view.

When the contents are not highlighted and the field is not blank, pressing the UP ARROW and DOWN ARROW keys have no effect, and the RIGHT ARROW and LEFT ARROW keys move within the field for editing.

To make it easier to navigate through forms, we'll refer to the fields by their label, not the field name. So we'll refer to the Company and the State/Province fields when viewing the form.

Press HOME to move to the first field. Now press ENTER twice to move to the Company text box, and then click on the Next Record button. The next record is displayed, with the same field automatically highlighted. Notice that the label for the Company Name field is just Company. You don't have to use the full field name on forms, as long as the label identifies the information you want to enter. When you type information into the text box, you are entering it into the Company Name field, regardless of the label. Also notice that the label for the StateOrProvince field is State/Province.

Now let's add a new record.

Click on either of the New Record buttons to display a new blank form. The form appears with the insertion point in the Company field. The insertion point remains in the current field when you move from record to record. Press the UP ARROW key twice to reach the first field. Type **Adam** and then press ENTER to reach the Last Name field. Type **Chesin** in the Last Name field, press ENTER, type **Chesin Pharmacy** in the Company field, press ENTER, and type **Adam** in the Dear field.

Press ENTER to reach the Address field, and notice that up and down arrows appear on the right of the text box. These indicate that the field can hold more than one line. You can move from line to line, after you've entered information into the field, by clicking on the arrows. Type **765 West Avenue** and then press CTRL-ENTER to move to the next line in the field. Type **Suite 305** and then press TAB to move out of the

Address field and into the City field. Type **Margate** in the City field, press ENTER, and then type **NJ** in the State/Province field.

Ensuring Valid Data with Input Masks

Now press ENTER or TAB to move to the Postal Code field and then type **0**, the first number of the zip code. When you start to type in the field, Access displays a mask indicating the format of the field.

This mask shows that the zip code is formatted to appear with a hyphen after the first five characters. This means that you don't have to type the hyphen yourself—Access has already inserted it for you. But there's more to the mask than that. A mask can also determine the number and types of characters that you can enter. (Format characters from the mask, such as the hyphen, are not saved with the data—they are just displayed to make things easier to read.)

Type **840** and then press ENTER before completing the code. Access shows a warning message that you did not enter the correct format. Click OK to clear the message box and then type **2** to complete the five characters of the code. The insertion point jumps to the other side of the hyphen. Now press ENTER to move to the Country field (you won't receive a warning message about completing the zip code information, because the last four numbers of the Postal Code input mask are optional). Type **USA** in the Country field, and **President** in the Title field.

In the Work Phone field, start by entering **6**. When you start typing the phone number, Access displays the field input mask. This shows that you enter a three-character area code, three numbers for the exchange, and the four final numbers. Access will insert the parentheses and the hyphen for you—you do not have to type them yourself, so complete the phone number by typing **096541248**. Now complete the fields by entering **763** as the Work Extension, (609) 654-1258 as the Home Phone, (609) 641-0976 as the Mobile Phone, and (609) 654-1259 as the Fax Number.

If you press ENTER after typing the fax number, the insertion point moves to the first field on the page. To start the second page of the form, click on the Page 2 button. You'll see that the contact name is

already filled in for you and that the text box is gray. Access combines the first name and last name you already entered to display the full name. This field is actually only displayed on the form, and it is not saved with the table. After all, why should it be? The first and last names are stored, so Access can combine them to display the full name whenever it needs to.

Picking Values with Lists

Look at the Contact Type field. It has a down arrow. Click on the arrow to see a lookup table containing the contact types that are stored in the Contact Types table. A lookup table makes it easy to enter information into a field, and it ensures that you do not enter a contact type that does not really exist. Click on Seller and then press ENTER to reach the EMAIL field. Type **achesin@shelly.com** and press ENTER twice to reach the Birthdate field. Where's the insertion point? It's at the right side of the field. Type **11**—the characters move to the left, and the date mask appears. Complete the date by typing **2245**. Access will move the day and year to the proper positions in the field.

Leave the remaining fields blank for now, and click on the Previous Record button. Moving to any other record saves the current one. The second page is displayed because it was displayed on the last record you worked with. Click on the Page 1 button.

CHANGING INFORMATION IN A FORM

The world is always changing, and so is the information in a database. Contacts move or change their phone numbers, prices go up and down, and inventory is always changing. Changing the information in your database is just as easy as entering it. In fact, it's easier, because you only have to update the fields that have changed.

To change information in a field, just go to its text box and type. When you move into a box using the keyboard (by pressing the TAB or ENTER keys, for example), the entire field will be selected. Pressing any other key will delete the contents so you can enter something else. To edit the contents without deleting it all first, press F2 to enter edit mode, or click in the field with the mouse. Then change the information just as you would edit text in a word processing program.

- Press BACKSPACE or DEL to erase characters.
- Press INS to change between insert and overtype mode. If the characters OVR appear in the status bar, new characters you type will erase those already there, otherwise they will be inserted between existing characters.
- Use the mouse to drag over characters that you want to select to delete or cut and copy to other locations using the Cut, Copy, and Paste operations.

To see how Access works, let's change some information in the first record.

1. Click on the First Record button to move to the record for Nancy Davolio.
2. Click in the Company Name field and replace the word Roasters with Incorporated.
3. Now click in the City field, and replace the word Seattle with Wallace.

Remember, a record is saved when you move to a new record or when you close the form. Since you did neither of these, the changes you just made are not yet saved on the disk. So if you change your mind about the changes, you can still do something about it. To undo your actions, you use the Undo button. This button serves a dual purpose:

- If you have not yet moved out of the field you just changed, click on the button to undo the change.
- If you have already moved out of the field, click on the button to return the entire record to its original contents.

DELETING RECORDS

Sometimes information changes so much that you no longer need it in the database. Members drop out, inventory goes out-of-stock, and employees move on to other companies. When you no longer need a record in the database, you should delete it. This saves you the trouble of scrolling through outdated records, and it saves space on your hard disk.

To delete an entire record, click on the Delete Record button in the toolbar. A dialog box will appear warning you that the record will be deleted. Click on Yes to actually delete the record. You can also delete a record by selecting it—clicking on the selection bar or choosing Select Record from the Edit menu—and then pressing DEL or choosing Cut from the Edit menu. To delete every record, choose Select All Records from the Edit menu and then press DEL.

SHORTCUT

Press CTRL-- (CTRL and the minus sign) to delete the current record.

SORTING RECORDS

The form determines the way your information is displayed but not its order. Seeing records in a particular order can help you find and analyze information. If you're a teacher, for example, it might be helpful to list students in grade order. It would certainly save you money to print a mailing list in zip code order to take advantage of bulk-rate postage. And it would also be much easier to locate items if they appeared in alphabetical order.

The order in which records appear as you move from one to the other depends on how the table was created. If the table has a primary key, then the records will appear in primary key order. (Let's save time and be informal, and we'll just call it the key from now on.) For example, in the Contacts table, the key is the Contact ID field—the number that Access enters as you create new records. As you move from record to record, the number in the Go to Record box matches the Contact ID number. Because the ID is the key, it just so happens that the ID and Go to Record number are the same. The ID, however, is solely based on the order in which you entered the records—probably in the order that clients signed on.

definition

Key: A field or combination of fields used to determine the order of records in the table. A key makes it easier and faster to find records and to perform many other database functions.

When you want to display the records in some other order, you sort them. Sorting does not change the physical order in which the records are stored on your disk; it changes only the order in which the records are displayed on the screen. And sorting does not change the key.

The fastest way to sort the information is to use the Sort Ascending and Sort Descending buttons in the toolbar. First, place the insertion point in the field you want to sort by. If you want to display records by

Sorting also works sort of the same in Datasheet View.

SHORTCUT

You can also select Sort Ascending and Sort Descending from the shortcut menu that appears when you click the right mouse button on a field.

If you want to sort on more than one field, you must use the Advanced Sort feature. We'll show you how in Chapter 3.

the client's last name, for example, click in the Last Name field. To sort by zip code, click in the Postal Code field. Then click on either Sort Ascending or Sort Descending, depending on the order that you want.

Let's try it now:

1. If the first record is not already displayed, click on the First Record button. The record number and the Contact ID read 1.
2. Now click on the Last Name field and then on the Sort Descending button.

That's it—the records are sorted. The record for Peacock now comes first, as you can see by the number 1 in the record counter. But notice that the Contact ID says 4, which are the actual contents of the field. Click on the Last Record button. Buchanan's record is the last of 6, but his Contact ID number is 5. As you move from record to record, the record number increments but the order no longer matches the Contact ID. That's fine. It just means that you are viewing the records in some other order than their key.

Let's try another sort:

1. Click on the Page 2 button and then on the Birthdate field.
2. Now click on Sort Ascending.

The records are now sorting in date order, with the oldest date first.

Since you cannot click on the Contact ID field on the form, you cannot sort records on that field. It doesn't matter, because that is the key field. To return the records to their original order, select Remove Filter/Sort from the Records menu. The record number and the Contact ID fields will now match.

FILTERING RECORDS

While sorting changes the order in which records are displayed, scrolling through the table will still display all of the records. There are plenty of times, however, when you're only interested in certain ones,

Filter: *Something that keeps something else out; or one or more conditions that a record must meet in order to be displayed.*

such as clients who owe you a lot of money or customers who have not ordered this year. To display specific records, you apply a filter.

When you make coffee, the paper filter lets the coffee through to the pot while keeping back the grinds. It determines what makes it into the pot. An Access filter determines which records make it to the screen. A filter does not delete records from the database. Those not meeting the conditions will not be displayed, but they are still part of the database.

There are three ways to filter records: by selecting, by form, and by using an advanced filter that you'll learn about in Chapter 3. All three methods work the same with forms and with datasheets.

upgrade note

Filter by Selection and Filter by Form are two great additions to Access for Windows 95. If you use filters, take some time to review these new features. They'll save you a lot of time.

Filter by Selection

In Filter by Selection, you select a field already containing the information you want to use for the condition. For example, if you want to display contacts in Washington, click on any of the State/Province fields for a Washington contact. To display all contacts who are buyers, click on the Contact Type field for a buyer. Once you've selected the field, click on the Filter By Selection button.

Try it now. First, choose Remove Filter/Sort from the records menu to return the forms to their original order. Click on the State/Province field of the displayed record, and then click on the Filter By Selection button. The record counter will show you the number of records that meet the criteria, and it will remind you that you are looking at a filtered view of the table, as in:

Now as you move from record to record, only those meeting the filter condition will appear—a subset of the entire table. You will only

see contacts in the same state as the selected record. If you now select another field for the filter, only those from the subset will be considered. This way, you can filter on the contents of more than one field, but just one field at a time.

To apply a new filter to the entire table, you must remove the filter. In the toolbar, you'll see this button pressed down:

When pressed down it is called Remove Filter, when not pressed it is called Apply Filter. Click on that button now, or select Remove Filter/Sort from the Records menu. With the filter removed, all of the records will now be included.

Filter by Excluding

Filter by Selection excludes all records that do not match the contents of the selected field. But what if you want to see all records except those that meet a condition, such as the records for all clients who are not in Washington? To exclude specific records from the filter, use the Filter Excluding Selection command.

To do this, click on a field containing the information that you want to use to exclude records—just the opposite of Filter by Selection. Then right-click on the field and choose Filter Excluding Selection from the shortcut menu that appears.

Filter by Form

The problem with Filter by Selection is that you must first find one record with the information you want to use for the filter. If you are looking for a contact in Redmond, for instance, you must find one first. And, if you want to filter on the contents of more than one field—say contacts in Redmond, Washington, but not Redmond, New Jersey—you must perform each filter separately.

Filter by Form solves both problems. When you filter by form, Access displays a form like that shown in Figure 2.3. The fields will be blank except for any conditions you last used for a filter. Since you just filtered the records in Washington state, "WA" appears in the State/Province field. You fill in the fields with the information that you want to use for the filter.

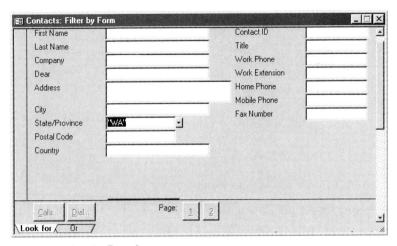

Figure 2.3 Filter by Form form

Let's try it:

1. Click on the Filter By Form button to display a blank form.

2. Click in the State/Province field. See the down arrow? It represents a drop-down list.
3. Click on the arrow to see a list of the states already in the table. Rather than type the information yourself, just select from the list.
4. Click on NJ to select as the filter condition.
5. Now click on the Apply Filter button. Only New Jersey contacts will be included in the subset.

You can enter conditions in as many fields as you want, so you can filter on multiple fields in one operation.

1. Click on the Filter By Form button again. The form appears with the criteria you've already entered.
2. Click on the City field.

Drop-down list: *A list of options from which you can choose, indicated by a down arrow that appears on the right of a text box.*

3. Pull down the list and select Redmond.
4. Click in the State/Province field.
5. Pull down the list and select WA.
6. Now click on the Apply Filter button. Only contacts in Redmond, Washington, will be included in the subset.

Click on Filter By Form once more and look at the bottom of the form—at the OR button. When you enter information in more than one field, Access treats it as an AND operation. This means that the record must match all of the conditions in the form—both Redmond in the City field and WA in the State field. What if you wanted to list contacts in either Redmond, Washington or New Jersey? This is called an OR operation. To add an OR condition, you need to use another form.

1. Click on the OR button at the bottom of the form. A blank form appears (with another dimmed OR button).
2. Click on the State/Province field, pull down the list, and select NJ.
3. Apply the filter.

The subset now includes contacts in Redmond, Washington, and in any city in New Jersey.

You can have more than one OR condition. Just click on the dimmed OR button to display another form. If you have the spare time, keep on clicking on the dimmed OR button to see just how many conditions you can have (we got to 25 and then gave up).

Removing the filter redisplays all of the records. However, it does not erase the criteria from the filter form. The next time you open the form—even after closing and reopening the database—the last-used criteria will appear in the filter form. Try this out. Click on the Remove Filter button so the table is no longer filtered. Now click on the Filter By Form button. The criteria are still there in the City and State/Province fields. To erase the filter criteria, click on the Clear Grid button and then on the Apply Filter button.

Unless you clear the grid, the last applied filter is stored with the table as something called a property. *Store that away until you read Chapter 7.*

When you enter a value into a field box or select one from the list, Access looks for an exact match. If you type CA in the State/Province field, for example, the record must contain CA to be included in the filtered set. You can also search for less exact matches using wildcards and comparison operators. This is pretty much the usual Windows stuff. In fields that contain text, use the wildcards ? and *. The question mark represents any one character, so if you enter ?A in the State/Province field, records containing PA, CA, and MA will be in the set, as well as any others with one letter followed by the letter A. The asterisk represents any number of characters. The notation Sm*, for example, means any text starting with the letters SM and followed by any other characters, such as Smith, Smyth, and Smoot.

In fields that contain numbers, use these comparison operators:

<	less than
>	greater than
<=	less than or equal to
>=	greater than or equal to
<>	not equal to

For example, entering <5 in the Client ID field will include only the first four clients in the filtered set.

To end your session, click on the Close button in the Filter By Form window. You can now work with your form, return to the database window, or exit Access.

SO WHAT'S NEXT?

When you want to see more than one record on the screen at a time, use the Datasheet View, the topic of Chapter 3.

DO NOT DISTURB

Using Datasheets-
Almost Instant and Others

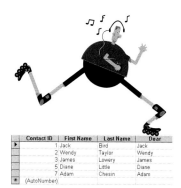

FAST FORWARD

DISPLAY A TABLE IN DATASHEET VIEW ➤ *pp 49-51*

- Double-click on the table in the Tables page of the database window.

SELECT FIELDS,
RECORDS, AND COLUMNS ➤ *pp 51-52*

- To select a record, click on the record selector.
- To select consecutive records, drag over the record selectors, or select the first record and then SHIFT-click on the last record.
- To select a column, click on the column selector.
- To select consecutive columns, drag over the column selectors, or select the first column and then SHIFT-click on the last column.
- To select a record's field, click on the gridline to the left of the field. Drag over to select multiple fields.

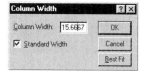

CHANGE THE WIDTH OF COLUMNS ➤ *pp 52-53*

Drag the line following the field name, double-click on the line following the field name, or follow these steps:

1. Click anywhere in the column that you want to adjust, or select multiple columns.
2. Choose Column Width from the Format menu.
3. Click on Best Fit, enter width in characters, or select Standard Width.

CHANGE THE HEIGHT OF ROWS ➤ *p 54*

Drag a line between any record selector, or follow these steps:

1. Click on the row.
2. Choose Row Height from the Format menu.
3. Choose Standard Height or enter the height in points.

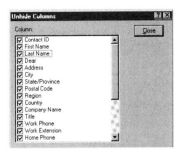

HIDE AND UNHIDE COLUMNS ➤ *pp 54-55*

To hide columns, select the column that you want to hide, then choose Hide Columns from the Format menu.

To unhide columns,

1. Choose Unhide Columns from the Format menu.
2. Click on the empty check box next to hidden field names.
3. Close the dialog box.

FREEZE COLUMNS ➤ *pp 55-56*

1. Click in any field in the column.
2. Choose Freeze Columns from the Format menu.

To unfreeze columns, choose Unfreeze All Columns from the Format menu.

CHANGE THE ORDER OF COLUMNS ➤ *p 56*

1. Select the column that you want to move by clicking its field name, or drag across the field names to select multiple columns.
2. Point to selected columns.
3. Drag to the column that you want to follow the selected one(s).

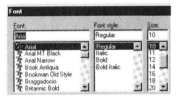

CHANGE THE DATASHEET FONT ➤ *pp 56-57*

- Choose Font from the Format menu and choose a font, style, size, and color.

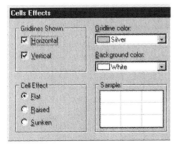

FORMAT THE DATASHEET ➤ *pp 57-59*

Select Cells from the Format menu, then:

- Choose to display horizontal and vertical gridlines.
- Select line color.
- Choose cell background color.
- Select flat, raised, or sunken effect.

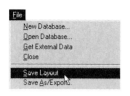

SAVE A MODIFIED DATASHEET LAYOUT ➤ *pp 59-60*
- Choose Save Layout from the File menu.

SWITCH FROM FORM VIEW
TO DATASHEET VIEW ➤ *pp 60-61*
- When the form is displayed, click on the View button and select Datasheet View.

PERFORM AN ADVANCED
FILTER AND SORT ➤ *pp 63-64*
1. Display the datasheet or form for the table.
2. Open the Records menu, point to Filter, and then click on Advanced Filter/Sort.
3. Double-click on the fields from the field list to insert them into the grid.
4. Select sort options.
5. Enter criteria for filtering.
6. Click on Apply Filter.

Forms are nice to look at, and easy to use. They are great for entering information, but you can't get an overall look at your data. Sometimes you might just like to see what's already in your table as you enter a new record or edit an existing one. That's when you use the *datasheet*, which can display a number of records all at one time. Glancing through the table in a datasheet can often give you ideas, helping you fill out the record you're working on. It's a great time-saver for us busy folks, so we're sure you'll find the datasheet useful for many reasons—even if it doesn't look as pretty as a form.

DISPLAYING A DATASHEET

To display a datasheet, just open a table from the database window. It's as quick as that. Try it now. Start Access, open the Contacts database as you learned to do in Chapter 1, and display the database window. Click on the Tables tab to see the tables that are part of the database. Now click on the Contacts table and select Open.

What you're looking at is called a datasheet. The gray area to the left of the first field is the *record selector*. The triangle indicates the current record—the record that would be deleted if you clicked on the Delete Record button, for example. The asterisk next to the blank row at the end of the table means that the row will be used for the next record you add. There is not actually a blank record on the table.

Current record ———————▶

Next new record ———————▶

Record selector

Contacts : Table					
Contact ID	First Name	Last Name	Dear	Address	Ci
1	Nancy	Davolio	Nancy	507 - 20th Ave.	Wallace
2	Janet	Leverling	Janet	722 Moss Bay E	Kirkland
3	Andrew	Fuller	Andrew	908 W. Capital '	Tacoma
4	Margaret	Peacock	Margaret	4110 Old Redm	Redmor
5	Steven	Buchanan	Steve	14 Garrett Hill	London
6	Adam	Chesin	Adam	765 West Avent	Margate
*	(AutoNumber)				

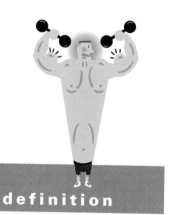

definition

Datasheet: A representation of the information in a table in rows and columns; field names are the column headings, and each row represents a record.

♪ ♪

That's one of the problems with datasheets—you can't see too many fields at a time.

Now for some standard Windows stuff. If you can't see all of the fields on screen, there'll be a scroll bar next to the record navigation buttons. There'll also be a scroll bar down the right if not all records are displayed. To move around the datasheet, just click where you want to add or edit information, scrolling as needed. If you're not into mice, you can move through the datasheet using the keystrokes listed in Table 3.1. It's up to you, but we usually find a combination of mouse and keyboard to be best. For example, you can use keys like TAB, HOME, END, and the arrow keys to travel around consecutive fields and rows, and the mouse when moving about at random.

Keypress	Description
PGUP	Up one page of records
PGDN	Down one page of records
CTRL-PGUP	Left one page of fields
CTRL-PGDN	Right one page of fields
TAB	To the next field
SHIFT-TAB	To the previous field
HOME	To the first field in the current record
END	To the last field in the current record
UP ARROW	To the same field in the previous record
DOWN ARROW	To the same field in the next record
CTRL-UP ARROW	To the same field on the first record
CTRL-DOWN ARROW	To the same field in the last record

Table 3.1 Keypresses to Use to Move Around the Database

Déjà Vu

Now look at the toolbar and the record navigation buttons. They are exactly the same as in Form View. In fact, all of the techniques for moving among records and for adding, sorting, filtering, and deleting records work exactly the same in either Form View or Datasheet View. As one of our presidents was known to say, let us make this perfectly clear. To recap:

See Appendix B if you need help using the scroll bars or another part of the Windows interface.

- *To add a new record*, either click on the New Record button or move into the blank row and enter the data.
- *To enter or edit information*, move to the field and type, just as you learned to do for a form.
- *Sort the datasheet* by clicking in the column you want to sort by, and then click on Sort Ascending or Sort Descending.
- *Filter the datasheet by selection*, excluding selection, or by form, exactly as you learned in Chapter 2. When you click on Filter By Form, Access displays a blank datasheet where you enter or select the filter information. You'll also be able to select information from a drop-down list, just as you can from a form.
- *To delete a record*, click on any of its fields and then click on the Delete Record button. To delete several records, select them first. You can also select the row or rows, and then press DEL.
- All of the same *shortcut keys* work: CTRL-+ (CTRL and the plus sign) to add a record; CTRL- − (CTRL and the minus sign) to delete a record; ESC to undo; CTRL-' (CTRL and an apostrophe) to copy the cell contents from the previous record; SHIFT-ENTER to save the record.

If you feel like entering new records without seeing existing ones, choose Data Entry from the Records menu. When you're ready to look at the entire datasheet again, choose Remove Filter/Sort from the Records menu.

SELECTING FIELDS AND RECORDS

Working with information is a two-step dance—you first select what you want to deal with, and then you do something with it.

To select a record, point to the record selector next to the record so the mouse pointer appears as a black right-pointing arrow, and then

SHORTCUT

Press CTRL-A to select all the records.

Use the same techniques to select entire columns; just point to the field name so the mouse pointer appears like a black down arrow.

Select consecutive fields in a row, such as City and State, to filter and sort on multiple fields at one time using an AND condition. Select fields in consecutive rows to filter and sort using an OR condition.

To change the column any other size, even narrower than the column heading, drag the line with the mouse; drag to the left to make the column smaller and to the right to make it wider.

click—the entire record will become highlighted. To select several consecutive records, select the first record, then hold down the SHIFT key and click on the last record in the group. You can also drag to select: point to the first record selector so the pointer appears like the arrow, hold down the mouse button and drag down to the last record. To select every record, open the Edit menu and choose Select All Records.

You can also select entire fields when you want to delete their contents or use them for filters and sorts. Point to the line to the left of the field so the pointer appears like a large plus sign and then click. All of the text in the field will be selected, as well as any blank space following the text. To select more than one field—even if they are in different records—drag the plus sign pointer or select the first field in the group and then SHIFT-click on the last field.

GETTING THE MOST FROM YOUR COLUMNS

Column width can be a real dilemma—either feast or famine. Sometimes you can't see all of the information in a field, for example in the Address field. Sometimes you see what looks like wasted space, as in the Dear and the State/Province fields.

A handy solution is Best Fit. Best Fit makes a column just as wide as its largest entry (including the field name), and it's quick—just double-click on the line following the field name. For example, to see the full address, double-click on the line following the Address field name. Access will widen the column. If you now apply Best Fit to the Dear column, however, Access will narrow the column to minimize the amount of blank space following the short field entries.

If you want to set the column width to an exact number of characters, then click anywhere in the column you want to adjust, or select several columns to adjust them all at the same time, then choose Column Width from the Format menu to see this dialog box:

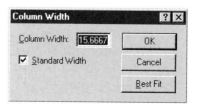

habits & strategies

Because you cannot cancel layout changes with the Undo command, save your table layout after each change that you find successful.

You can enter a new column width in characters, return to the standard width, or have Access adjust the column for you with the Best Fit option.

By the way, don't bother trying Best Fit on the State/Province field to eliminate the spaces after the state abbreviations. The Best Fit option will not make a column narrower than the field name. You can make the column narrower by dragging, but then you won't see the complete heading. The choice is yours; however, we'd rather see more columns on the screen, even if some field names are not complete. After all, it doesn't take much of a genius to guess what the two-letter abbreviations represent.

It's usually a waste of time to widen all of your columns to best fit, anyway. There are some columns that you don't use that often in Datasheet View, like the Address field. When you want to enter or edit an address or any field that doesn't fit in a column, use the Zoom box, as explained in the following steps. This saves you the trouble of widening a column you do not use that often, saving you some scrolling time. The Zoom box is a like a mini word processor. As you type, your text will wrap when it reaches the right margin, and there'll be a scroll bar to scroll through a really long field.

USING THE ZOOM BOX step by step

1. Move to the field you want to enter, edit, or view, and press SHIFT-F2.

2. Enter or edit the text, as needed.

3. Click on OK.

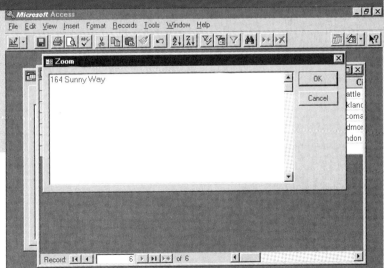

DISPLAYING MORE INFORMATION IN ROWS

If you don't want to widen a column to see a long field, you can try increasing the height of the rows. (For us, it's the only reason to change row height.) Of course, while this displays more information in the same column space, you'll see fewer records on screen at a time. Life's just full of decisions. You can't change the height of an individual row, only all of them at the same time. Still, it's a good alternative to using the Zoom box. It can also be faster, since the Zoom box only displays one field at a time, and you have to open and close the Zoom box each time you want to see another field. By increasing the row height, you see the full contents of several records at a time. And because you widen every row with just one action, it's pretty fast.

To change row height by dragging, point to a line between any record selector and drag—up for shorter rows, down for taller ones. When you release the mouse, all of the rows will be set at the new height. To set a specific height, or to quickly return to the default, choose Row Height from the Format menu. Then in the dialog box that appears, enter the row height in points (there are 72 points to an inch) or click on Standard Height.

The standard height is always slightly larger than the font size used for the text.

DISPLAYING IMPORTANT FIELDS

One other way to see more fields on the screen is to hide columns that you're not interested in at the moment. For example, in the Contacts database there are no entries in the region field. If you do not plan on using a field for a time, you can hide it from being displayed. You can hide as many columns as you want. If you want to scan the datasheet for names and telephone numbers, for example, you can hide all but those two fields.

Here's how. Select the column that you want to hide, and then select Hide Columns from the Format menu. The column will no longer appear on screen but it still is part of the table. The information is still there and you can get back just as easily. To unhide columns, select Unhide Columns (what else?) from the Format menu.

CAUTION

Hiding doesn't delete the field and its information, it just prevents the field from being displayed. Deleting a column actually erases the information from the database.

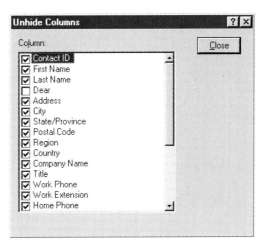

Access displays a list of the fields with check marks next to those that are displayed. The check boxes of hidden columns will be empty. To unhide a column, click on its check box and then on Close.

FREEZING COLUMNS FOR EASY REFERENCE

Scrolling to see fields can be a pain, but having to scroll back and forth is torture. It's hard to avoid. In most databases, the first field or two identifies the record—usually a number, name, or some other piece of information that tells what the record is all about. As you scroll more columns into view, the identifying fields scroll off the left edge of the screen. So when you are typing the Work Phone for the Contacts table, for example, you won't see the ID or name for the record you are adding.

The solution is to freeze the identifying columns so you'll always know which record you are working with. Freezing is a great time-saver when you're either adding or editing records. (It saves a lot of time, trust us.) To freeze a column, click in any field within it, or select multiple columns when you want to freeze more than one, then select Freeze Columns from the Format menu. Access moves the columns to the left of the screen—if they were not there before—and selects them. Click the mouse to unselect the columns. The frozen columns will be separated from the rest by a solid line. Now as you scroll, the frozen columns will remain in view.

*Select multiple columns using the SHIFT
key or by dragging to move them all at
the same time.*

*Changing the order of columns does
not change the actual table itself—just
its layout in the datasheet. Remember,
the datasheet is not THE table, just one
way of looking at it.*

To unfreeze the columns, select Unfreeze All Columns from the Format menu. The column is no longer frozen. Quick and easy, but there's a catch. The unfrozen (or is it unfreezed?) columns stay right there at the far left of the table, even if they were not there originally. If you want to move the columns back to their original position, read on.

CHANGING THE ORDER OF COLUMNS

You can change the order of fields in the datasheet to make it more convenient to enter or edit information or to select consecutive fields for sorting or filtering. For example, if you want to sort on the State and Contact type fields, you can place them together so you can select and sort on both at one time.

To change the order of fields, select the column that you want to move by clicking its field name. Point to the field name—in any of the selected columns—so the pointer appears like an arrow, and then hold down the mouse button. If you did it correctly, you'll see a small rectangle below the mouse pointer and a vertical line to the left of the column. Drag the mouse to where you want to move the column and then release the mouse button.

CHANGING THE DATASHEET FONT

Now you're ready for the fancy stuff. You can change the way your datasheet looks by choosing a new text font. Your selections affect the entire table. Sorry, Microsoft doesn't trust us to format individual cells, columns, or rows. When a datasheet is displayed, choose Font from the Format menu to see the dialog box shown in Figure 3.1. Select the font, its size and style of characters, whether you want it underlined, and its color. For some fonts you can also choose a script to select characters other than Western. Some options are Greek, Turkish, and Hebrew.

*The default font is Arial
10-point Regular.*

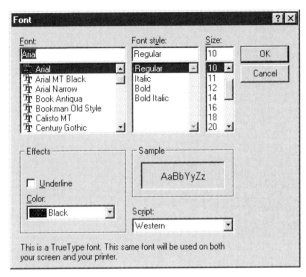

Figure 3.1 Font dialog box

CHANGING THE APPEARANCE OF CELLS

habits & strategies

As you select options, keep an eye on the sample or preview section. Make sure the sample looks right before accepting the settings.

upgrade note

The ability to format the cells and lines of the datasheet is a new feature. You can now format the datasheet for a more attractive onscreen display and printout. The formats affect the entire datasheet, not individual lines or cells.

While you'll probably be printing information in a form or report, datasheets are good for viewing a number of records on the screen. If you are using the datasheet to give a presentation, even if it is for just one important person, then you can format its appearance for a more professional look.

To format the datasheet, choose Cells from the Format menu to see the dialog box shown in Figure 3.2. Here you can choose to display the horizontal and vertical gridlines, change their color and the cell background, and format cells as flat (the default), or with a raised or sunken look, perhaps to suit your mood at the time. You can only select which gridlines to show, by the way, when using the flat cell effect.

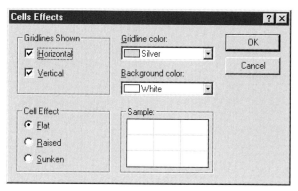

Figure 3.2 Cells Effects dialog box

Some color and effect combinations can really look terrible, and they can even make your table unreadable. If you select a combination that looks like a cheap tie, return to the defaults by clicking on the same Cell Effect option in the dialog box. Access will automatically restore the default settings.

Using the Formatting Toolbar

As an alternative to the Font and Cells Effects dialog boxes, you can use a special toolbar. While it may seem easier to use a toolbar, we think the sample panels in the dialog boxes give them the edge. With the dialog boxes, you can look at the sample panel to see how your choices will affect the cells. So, you can always continue selecting until it looks right, or select Cancel in the dialog box to scrap the whole thing. There's no preview using the toolbar. If you change your mind about a selection, you must select something else from the same toolbar list. Of course, you can always display the Cells Effects dialog box and click on the effect to reset it to the default, but then you're using the dialog box anyway.

When you're looking at a datasheet, point to any place in the toolbar that is displayed and click the *right* mouse button to see this menu:

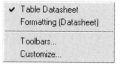

CAUTION

Changes to the layout cannot be undone with the Undo button or the Undo command from the Edit menu.

From the shortcut menu, click on Formatting (Datasheet) to see the toolbar shown here:

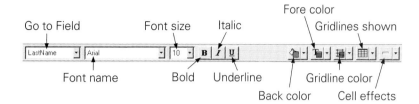

Use the Go to Field box, which shows the name of the current field, to move from column to column. Pull down the list and select the field you want to move to. The other buttons and lists in the toolbar change the appearance of the entire table, just like their corresponding options in the dialog boxes. The toolbar will automatically be removed when you leave Datasheet View, but it will reappear when you look at another datasheet. To remove the toolbar yourself, right-click on any toolbar and then click on Formatting (Datasheet) again.

SOME THINGS TO AVOID AT THIS STAGE OF THE GAME

As you go boldly forth into the exploration of Access, you'll see some options on menus—regular or shortcut—that you should avoid for now. It's not that you won't need them; it's just that choosing them could create problems that you're not quite ready yet to handle, especially if you're taking advantage of forms and reports in an Almost Instant Database. So for now, avoid renaming, deleting, and inserting columns. These options actually affect the table, not just the appearance of the datasheet.

SAVING YOUR NEW LAYOUT

When you add or edit information to the table, Access saves your change automatically. If you make any changes to the layout of the datasheet, you must save them yourself. After adjusting the datasheet, click on the Save button in the toolbar, or choose Save Layout in the File menu.

If you do not save the layout, Access will display a message asking if you want to save it when you close the datasheet. Select Yes to save the change or No to cancel them. Close the datasheet now, saving any changes that you've made if you like how they appear.

SWITCHING BETWEEN FORMS AND DATASHEETS

When you're looking at a form, you can quickly switch to a datasheet without going through the database window. It's not the same datasheet that you see when you open a table, but it's a datasheet nonetheless.

When you open a form you are in Form View, looking at your information through a form. To change views, use the View button and drop-down arrow on the far left of the toolbar. The picture on the button represents the view you will switch to when you click on the button.

When looking at a form, the button is always named Form View, regardless of the current view.

![Design View icon]	Design View	In this view you can change the appearance of the form
![Form View icon]	Form View	This view displays the form

To choose a view not displayed on the face of the button, click on the down arrow next to the button and select a view from this list:

Not all views will be available at all times. If you pull down the list and select Datasheet View, you'll see a datasheet. Is it the same datasheet as you used before by opening the table? Not at all. When you switch to Datasheet View from a form, the datasheet has just the fields that were in the form, and in the same order as in the form, and not as in the original table. So the fields in this datasheet are in a different order than they were when you opened the datasheet from the database window, and any layout changes that you have applied do not appear. Still, it's a datasheet and you can work with the information just as you did from the datasheet before.

To switch out of Datasheet View, click on the down arrow and select Form View. You can now close the form to return to the database window.

GETTING MORE CONTROL WITH FILTERS

Choices, choices, and even more choices. In Chapter 2, you learned how to filter records by selection and by form. There's yet another way to filter that actually gives you more control over the process. It's called Advanced Filter/Sort. This command lets you filter and sort in one operation, on more than one field at a time, and using a wide range of criteria to select records.

You can use the Advanced Filter/Sort command when either a datasheet or form is displayed; however, you'll notice the results more immediately in a datasheet.

Selecting Records with the Grid

The Advanced Filter/Sort command lets you select records using criteria and also sort the records at the same time. To illustrate how the feature works, we'll be using the Calls table, which contains records of 16 calls (we're not sure if they are calls in or out, but it really doesn't matter). Our filter will display a list of calls concerning coffee, sorted by contact, but showing the most recent call for each first. It seems like quite a job, but it is easy with the grid.

1. Open the table you want to filter and sort (in this case, the Calls table).
2. Pull down the Records menu, point to Filter, and then click on Advanced Filter/Sort to see the grid, shown in Figure 3.3.

At the top of the grid window is a box containing a list of the fields in the Calls table. (The box will contain all of the fields from whatever table is being used, even if not all of the fields appear in the form being displayed.) On the bottom is the grid itself. You use the grid to determine the fields and criteria that you want to use for the filter. Each field that

The Advanced Filter/Sort command introduces something called the grid. You'll have to face the grid when you design queries later on, so learning about it now may make learning how to query that much easier.

The grid looks exactly the same if you display it from a form.

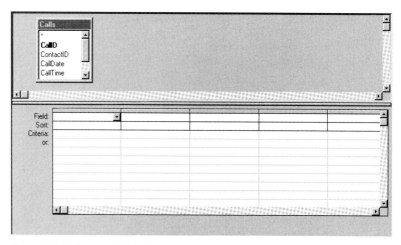

Figure 3.3 Advanced Filter/Sort grid

you want to use for a filter or for a sort must be in another column in the grid, in the field row.

> 3. Double-click on the fields you want to use for criteria or sorting. When you double-click on a field, Access inserts it into the first blank column in the Field row. You can also drag the field to the first empty cell in the Field row, or click in the first empty cell and then select the field from the drop-down list that appears. For example, here's our filter for the Calls table after inserting the Subject, ContactID, CallDate, and CallTime fields.

To remove a field from the grid, click on the gray bar above field name and press DEL.

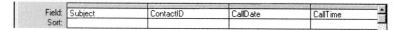

> 4. Click in the criteria row for a field that you want to use to select records, and enter a criterion just as you learned for Filter by Forms in Chapter 2. Sorry, you cannot select a value from a drop-down list. In this example, we've entered *coffee* to display calls that contain the word "coffee"; Access enters the word "Like" and the quotation marks after you press ENTER:

Remember, each asterisk means "any other characters," so in this case, it means any record that contains the characters "coffee", no matter where they appear in the field.

To return from the filtered datasheet to the grid, open the Window menu and choose the filter. It will be listed as something like CallsFilter1: Filter, referencing the table name.

Field:	Subject	ContactID	CallDate	CallTime
Sort:				
Criteria:	Like "*coffee*"			
or:				

5. To sort on a field, click on the Sort cell for the field, pull down the list that appears and choose from Ascending, Descending, and [None]. In our example, we're sorting by the ContactID in Ascending order and by the CallDate in Descending order, as shown here:

Field:	Subject	ContactID	CallDate	CallTime
Sort:		Ascending	Descending	
Criteria:	Like "*coffee*"			
or:				

6. Click on the Apply Filter button. The datasheet appears with only those records meeting the criteria and sorted just as you want.

Applying a filter to a table—by selection, by form, or advanced—is treated as a change to the table layout. When you close the table, a dialog box will appear asking if you want to save the changes. If you choose to save the changes, the filter will automatically be applied when you next open the table.

Creating Complex Filters and Sorts

As you learned in Chapter 2, criteria can be simple or they can be complex using AND or OR operations. The same goes for advanced filters and sorts. Access treats criteria in more than one field—in the Criteria row of the grid—as an AND operation. You can create OR conditions in a field or across fields using the OR row in the grid.

To create an OR operation in the same field, enter criteria such as *sell* or *buy*. If you want to list calls made in January and February, for example, use a criteria such as Between 1/1/95 and 2/28/95. Access will surround the date with # symbols. This is Access's way of identifying the characters as a date and not as two division operations.

You can also create an OR operation for a field, and even for different fields, using the OR row. For example, to list calls that had to

do with coffee and all calls on a certain date regardless of their subject, enter *coffee* in the criteria row under Subject, and enter the date in question in the OR row for the CallDate field.

Field:	Subject	ContactID	CallDate	CallTime
Sort:				
Criteria:	"coffee"			
or:			#12/13/94#	

SO WHAT'S NEXT?

You've got a lot of information in that database of yours. In Chapter 4, you'll learn quick ways to find and replace information, streamline data entry, correct your spelling, and print forms, reports, and datasheets.

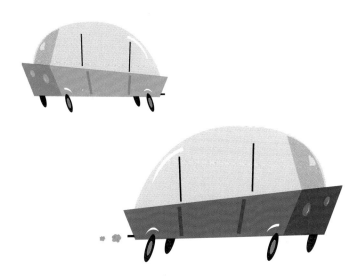

Finding, Correcting, and Printing Information

INCLUDES

- Finding and replacing information

- Streamlining data entry with AutoCorrect

- Checking your spelling

- Printing and previewing forms, reports, and datasheets

67

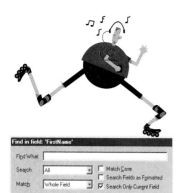

FAST FORWARD

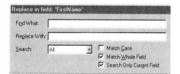

FIND INFORMATION IN THE TABLE ➤ *pp 70-72*

1. Click in the field containing the information you want to find.
2. Click on the Find button.
3. Type the text you want to locate.
4. Select Find options.
5. Click on Find First.
6. Click on Find Next until done.

REPLACE INFORMATION
AUTOMATICALLY ➤ *pp 73-74*

1. Click in the field containing the information you want to replace.
2. Choose Replace from the Edit menu.
3. Type the text you want to replace and press TAB.
4. Type the text you want to insert.
5. Select Search and Match options.
6. Click on Replace All, or click on Find Next and then Replace if desired.

CREATE AUTOCORRECT ENTRIES ➤ *pp 74-75*

1. Choose AutoCorrect from the Tools menu.
2. Enter the way you misspell a word, or an abbreviation you want to enter.
3. Press TAB.
4. Enter the correct spelling of the word, or the full text to replace the abbreviation.
5. Click on Add.
6. Click on OK.

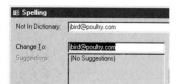

CHECK YOUR SPELLING ➤ *pp 75-78*

1. Select text, field, or records to check.
2. Click on the Spelling button.
3. Select appropriate dialog box options for each word.

PREVIEW FORMS, REPORTS, AND DATASHEETS ➤ *pp 79-80*

1. Select the object in the database window or open it on screen.
2. Click on Print Preview.
3. Click on Close when done.

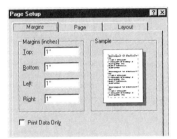

SET PAGE LAYOUT OPTIONS ➤ *pp 81-82*

1. Open the object for which you want to set the layout.
2. Choose Page Setup from the File menu.
3. Set the Layout, Page, and Margin options.
4. Close the dialog box.

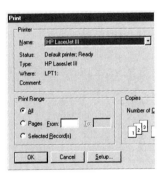

PRINT FORMS, REPORTS, AND DATASHEETS ➤ *pp 82-84*

1. Select the object in the database window or open it on screen.
2. Click on the Print button, or choose Print from the File menu and select Print options.

If you're anxious to print something and you can't wait till the section on printing in this chapter, just open what you want to print and click on the Print button in the toolbar. Feel better?

The Find command works the same whether you're looking for information in a form or in a datasheet.

habits & strategies

If you really do want to scan through records yourself, use a datasheet rather than a form. More records on the screen at a time means less scrolling.

You've covered a lot of material in the past three chapters, but there's still lots of ways that you can enhance the way you work with forms and datasheets. There are faster ways to find information in your database than by using the navigation keys, and there are better ways to change information, especially when making the same change to more than one record. And we're sure you'll want to print information in datasheets, forms, or reports, so you don't have to carry your computer everywhere you go!

FINDING INFORMATION

It can be really annoying when you can't find something. Your keys, your wallet, your car in the parking lot. You could get just as annoyed if you're looking for a particular item in a large table.

To find a specific record in a table, you can always use the Next Record and Previous Record buttons to scroll through the table one record at a time. This isn't a bad idea if you have a small table or you're not exactly sure what record you're looking for. But if you know what you're looking for—just not exactly where it is—then viewing every record is a serious waste of time. Rather than scan the table yourself, let Access do it with the Find command.

First, you have to know a piece of information contained in the record. For example, you could be looking for a contact whose last name is Fuller or for all contacts in Washington state or for any contact containing the word "chocolate" in the record.

If you know the field where the information is contained, start by placing the insertion point in that field, in any of the records, in either the datasheet or the form. So if you want to look for contacts in Washington, click in the State/Province field of any record, whether or not the state is Washington. If you don't know which field it's in—or don't care—the insertion point can be in any field. Then, click on the

Find button in the toolbar (the button that looks like a pair of binoculars) to see this dialog box:

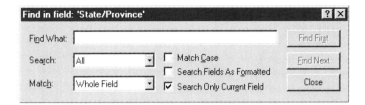

The title of the dialog box indicates that Access will look for information in the current field. That's fine. If you want to search all of the fields, just click on the Search Only Current Field option to deselect the check box. In the Find What box, you type what you're looking for. Next, decide how much of the table you want to search. Pull down the Search list and select one of the following:

- *Up* looks through records from the current one to the first.
- *Down* looks through records to the end of the table.
- *All* looks through all of the records.

The Match option determines where in the field the text must be. Your choices are Any Part of Field, Whole Field, and Start of Field. When set at Whole Field, Access only locates a record if the entire field is the same as the Find What entry. For example, if you type Chesin and search the Last Name field for a match on the Whole Field, Access won't find Chesin Pharmacy—the whole field contains more than just the name Chesin. If you select Any Part of Field, Access will locate records that contain the Find What characters no matter where they are. The purpose of the Start of Field options should be obvious.

The other two check boxes let you further control the search. Selecting Match Case means that the field must match the exact way you type the Find What text—uppercase for uppercase, lowercase for lowercase. Search Fields as Formatted is an interesting option. You can tell Access that you want some types of information to appear on the screen in a certain way, even though it is not actually stored on disk the same way. The best example is a date. Using techniques that you'll learn in Chapter 6, you can tell Access to display a date in a special format, say 10/22/45. When Access actually saves the date on the disk, it saves it as a code that takes up as few characters as possible

habits & strategies

You can only select Search Fields as Formatted if the Search Only Current Field option is also selected.

(you don't have to worry about that). When you do not search for a date as formatted, you can enter the Find What text in any other date format that Access understands. So searching for October 22, 1945 will locate a record containing 10/22/45. If you select this option, you must type the date as it appears on screen to locate it. This would be useful, for example, if you're looking for a specific reference to October 22, 1945 in a memo or text field.

Let's try the Find operation now using the Contacts table in your Contacts database. Suppose you want to locate contacts in the 206 area code, in any of the fields with a telephone number.

1. Open the Contacts database and then the Contacts table in datasheet view.
2. Scroll the table and click in the Work Phone field of the first record.
3. Click on the Find button.
4. Type **(206)** in the Find What box.
5. Since (206) is not the entire phone number, and you only want to find it when it comes at the start of the field, pull down the Match list and select Start of Field.
6. Click to select the Search Fields as Formatted option.
7. Click on Find First. Access moves to the first matching record, which is the current one in this case, and highlights the located text—(206).
8. Click on Find Next. Access highlights the next entry in the field that starts with the 206 area code.
9. Now click to deselect the Search Fields as Formatted option.
10. Click on Find Next. Since you're not looking for text formatted with parentheses, the entire field is now highlighted.
11. Click on Find Next one more time.
12. Now let's change the option to look for any phone number in that area code. Click on the Search Only Current Field box to deselect this option.
13. Click on Find Next again. Access moves to the Home Phone field of the same record.

Continue clicking on Find Next until you feel comfortable with the Find command, and then close the Find box.

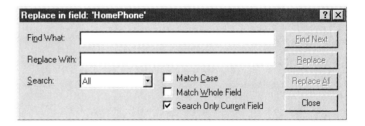

REPLACING INFORMATION AUTOMATICALLY

Replace works just like the same function in many word processing programs, such as Word for Windows. The only difference is that you can choose to replace text in any field, or in a specific field by placing the insertion point in it first.

Many times you search for information because you want to change it. So, it is a two-step process: find and then replace. There's an easier way to find and replace information, particularly when you want to make the same change in a number of records.

If you want to replace text in a particular field, then click in the field before you begin—either in a form or a datasheet. If you want to replace text no matter where it is, you can start in any field. Then select Replace from the Edit menu to see this dialog box:

Yes, Virginia, it is similar to the Find box, but there's some important differences. Type the text you want to replace in the Find What box, and type the text you want to insert in the Replace With box. Select a Search option: they are still All, Up, and Down. Match Case works the same as Find, as does the Search Only Current Field option; leave it selected to only replace text in the current field. The Match Whole Field option is now a separate check box, and an important one.

When you search for text, Access actually looks for the characters that you enter in the Find What text box, even if they are part of another word. So if you are searching for love (and who isn't?), Access will locate lovely, loveless, and even glove. If you select Match Whole Field, Access will only locate a match when the Find What text matches the entire entry in the field.

If you select Replace All, Access will first warn you that the action cannot be undone. Think carefully, and then select Yes if you want to continue. Access will then make all of the replacements for you. Automatically.

To play it safe, you should confirm each replacement before it is made. To do this, click on Find Next. Access will move to the first field that matches the Find What text and will highlight the text. If you want to make the replacement, click on Replace. Access makes the change and looks for the next occurrence. If you do not want to make the replacement, click on Find Next. To stop the operation, click on Close.

STREAMLINING DATA ENTRY WITH AUTOCORRECT

AutoCorrect is one of those great features that works so well, you sometimes don't even know it's there. In fact, it might have helped you already, without you even knowing it. AutoCorrect corrects mistakes automatically—that much is obvious by the name. If you mistakenly—or otherwise—type two capital letters for a word, for example, AutoCorrect changes the second to lowercase. If you forget to start the name of a day with an uppercase letter, AutoCorrect will do that for you, too.

AutoCorrect will also correct a whole bunch of common misspellings, such as replacing "acheive" with "achieve" and "yuor" with "your." But because most information in a database will usually be nouns (names, places, people, and things) and numbers, the built-in replacements of AutoCorrect may not be used that often. The real power of AutoCorrect, at least in Access, is that you can add AutoCorrect entries to correct your own common misspellings or to quickly insert text when you type an abbreviation for it. You create an AutoCorrect entry following the steps shown here.

Now whenever you misspell the word or type the abbreviation, Access will make the correction for you.

To see how AutoCorrect works, pull down the Tools menu and click on AutoCorrect to see the AutoCorrect dialog box. You can turn off each of the AutoCorrect options if you don't want them to be performed. For example, if you want to type day names with lowercase letters (although we can't think of a reason to do this), then click on Capitalize Names of Day to remove the check mark. To turn off the automatic replacement feature, deselect Replace Text as You Type.

When AutoCorrect is turned on, it will make the replacements shown in the list box. Scroll the list to see the type of corrections. You create your own AutoCorrect entries using the Replace and With text boxes. For example, suppose you commonly misspell the word "acid" as "asid." To have Access correct the mistake for you, type **asid** in the

Use the Delete button to remove the selected entry from the list.

CREATE AUTOCORRECT ENTRIES step by step

1. Select AutoCorrect from the Tools menu.

2. Enter the way you misspell a word, or an abbreviation you want to enter.

3. Press TAB.

4. Enter the correct spelling of the word, or the full text to replace the abbreviation.

5. Click on Add.

6. Click on OK.

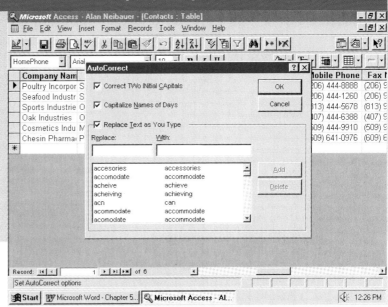

habits & strategies

Create AutoCorrect entries to help you enter names, places, and things that you frequently enter in the table.

If you've used the spelling checker in Word for Windows, then save some time and skip this section. The only difference is that you can select to ignore specific fields.

Replace box and **acid** in the With box. Then click on Add. Now when you type asid and press the SPACEBAR, ENTER, or TAB—which triggers AutoCorrect—Access will change its spelling to acid.

Now think about it. If Access replaces text as you type, why not use it to streamline your work? Getting tired of typing Los Angeles for all of your clients in the City of Angels? Type an abbreviation such as LA in the Replace box, and the full name in the With box. When you type LA in a field, Access automatically replaces it with Los Angeles, saving you quite a few keystrokes.

CHECKING YOUR SPELLING

Before printing your database forms or reports, especially if you're distributing them to VIPs, it's always a good idea to make sure that everything is spelled correctly.

The spelling feature works a lot like the one in Microsoft Word. It compares each word in the selected records against those in its dictionary. To begin checking your spelling, select what you want to check—the contents of a field, the entire record, or all of the records

—by choosing Select All Records from the Edit menu. Then click on the Spelling button in the toolbar (or press F7). When Access finds a word that is not in its dictionary, it displays the dialog box shown in Figure 4.1. The Not in Dictionary text box shows the word the way it is spelled in your table. If there are some suggested spellings in the Suggestions list box, the Change To prompt shows the selected word in the list. If Access cannot find any suggested spellings, the notation "(No Suggestions)" will appear in the list. You now have several options, depending on whether the word is spelled correctly or incorrectly.

The Ignore Field button is a new Microsoft feature. Click on this button when you want Access to ignore the entries in the named field for the remainder of the records. For example, since you know the EmailAddress field will contain some strange combinations of characters, click on Ignore "EmailAddress Field".

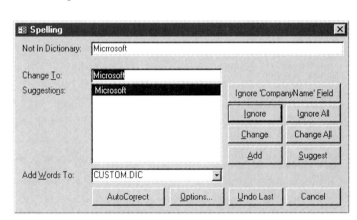

Figure 4.1 Use the Spelling feature to avoid embarrassments

When the Word Is Spelled Incorrectly

If you see the correct spelling in the list, double-click on it or select it and then choose either Change or Change All. Access inserts the correctly spelled word and then searches for the next error. When you choose Change, Access will report the next occurrence as a possible error so you can again select from the list. When you choose Change All, Access will automatically replace other occurrences of the same misspelling. Change All is useful when you know you've misspelled the same word in the same way several times in the same table.

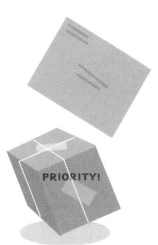

If you forget a space between words, as in MicrosoftAccess, the combination will be reported as not in the dictionary. Just edit or retype the words, with the space, in the Change To box and select Change.

If you do not see the correct spelling, or if no suggestions are listed, type another spelling for the word in the Change To box, and then click on either the Change button or the Suggest button, which becomes visible when you begin typing your new word. If you select Change, word looks in the dictionary for the new word; if it isn't there, Access will ask whether you want to use the replacement anyway and continue, or look up your replacement for possible alternatives. If you select Suggest, Access looks up the word you typed and displays alternative spellings for it.

The Change All option only affects the current spell check operation. If Access locates the same misspelling when checking another table or form, it will again report it as an error. When you know it's a word that you frequently misspell, click on the correct spelling in the list, or type it in the Change To box, and then click on the AutoCorrect button. Access will make the replacement in your document and create an AutoCorrect entry. Now whenever you type the incorrectly spelled word, AutoCorrect will replace it with the correct spelling.

When the Word Is Spelled Correctly

If the word is indeed spelled correctly, click on either Ignore or Ignore All. Access leaves the word as you typed it and continues the spell check. When you choose Ignore, Access will stop at the next occurrence and report it as a possible error. When you choose Ignore All, Access skips over all occurrences of the word in the table.

The Add option inserts the word into the custom dictionary so the same word will not be reported as misspelled in other tables.

More Spelling Choices

Now let's look at some other options in the Spelling dialog box.

If you select Change or Ignore by mistake, click on the Undo Last button to return to the previous word. If you've just changed the word, the original spelling will appear. Until you take some action in the Spelling dialog box, the Undo Last button will be dimmed.

To delete a word from the table, clear the contents of the Change To box. The Change and Change All buttons will change to Delete and Delete All. Select Delete to erase the single occurrence of the word; select Delete All to erase them all.

CAUTION

Undo Last does not work with the Delete All command.

Access ignores common pairs of duplicate words, such as "had had" and "that that."

If Access encounters two of the same correctly spelled words in a row, such as "do do," the second occurrence of the word is high-lighted and the Not in Dictionary box will be labeled Repeated Word. The Change To box will be empty. Choose Delete to erase the duplicate, or choose Ignore to leave it alone. To replace the word with another, type it in the Change To box—the Delete button will become Change so you can make the replacement.

Customizing Spelling

By default, the spelling checker ignores words in all uppercase characters and words that contain numbers. To change these and other spelling settings, click on Options in the Spelling dialog box to display the box shown in Figure 4.2.

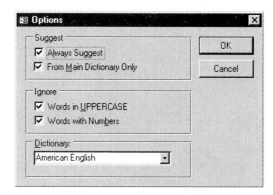

Figure 4.2 Set spelling options for the way you like to work

SHORTCUT

If you have a slower computer, there may be some delay as Word looks up suggested words. If you usually type the replacement word yourself, deselect the Always Suggest option. When you do want Word to find alternative spellings when checking a document, click on the Suggest button in the Spelling dialog box.

To proofread capitalized words and those that contain numbers, deselect the check boxes labeled Words in UPPERCASE and Words with Numbers. You can also choose whether Access automatically looks up suggested spellings by selecting or deselecting the Always Suggest check box. By default, Access will only show suggested spellings from the words in the main dictionary. If you want to see suggestions from your own custom dictionary, deselect the From Main Dictionary Only box. Access is sold worldwide so dictionaries are available for most languages. If you work in a multiple-language envi-ronment, you can purchase additional dictionaries and select which one you want to use by choosing it from the Dictionary list.

PREVIEWING FORMS, REPORTS, AND DATASHEETS

Paper may be cheap, but your time is not. There are not many things as frustrating as waiting for a long report or a series of forms to print, only to discover you've printed the wrong thing or just don't like the way it was printed. When it happens to us, our office looks like the bottom of a bird cage with discarded pages.

Before printing a form, report, or datasheet, you should check how the printout will appear using Print Preview. Now in some ways, Print Preview is a carryover from those ancient days, when dinosaurs roamed the earth and something called dBASE (yes, it is spelled oddly) was worshipped as a deity, and every character on the computer was the same size and font. Print Preview switched to a special graphics mode that displayed how a document would actually appear when printed, more or less.

To save typing, we'll just refer to Print Preview as Preview from now on.

With Windows, what you see on the screen is what gets printed, but Preview does have some special features, so it is not entirely a throwback to appease DOS Neanderthals. For example, you can see how much information prints on a page—how many forms or rows of the datasheet, for example—so you can make adjustments to the page layout before wasting your time and paper. You can preview a form or datasheet directly from the database window without opening it first.

Reports are always previewed, as there's no Open option for them anyway.

To preview a datasheet or form, for example, click on its name in the database window, and then click on the Print Preview button on the toolbar, or choose Print Preview from the File menu. The Access screen changes to the Preview mode, as shown in Figure 4.3. Now you see how your information will appear when printed and how much of the page it takes up. Access automatically prints the name of the object (the table, in this case) and the date at the top of the page and the page number at the bottom. Table 4-1 shows you what the Preview toolbar buttons are used for.

If the image is too small for you to see how the object really will look, point the mouse on the simulated page so the pointer appears like a magnifying lens, and then click. Access enlarges the display to 100 percent, the same size as it will be when printed. Click the mouse again to reduce the display so you see the whole page.

Click on Close when you're done looking at the preview.

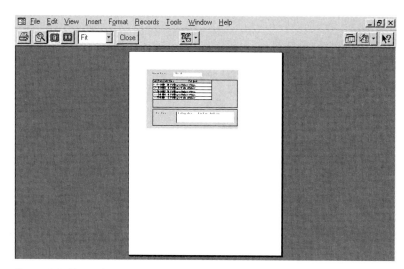

Figure 4.3 Forms in preview mode

Button	Name	Function
	Print	Prints the objects displayed in the Preview window
	Zoom	Toggles between enlarged and reduced display
	One Page	Shows one page at a time
	Two Pages	Shows two pages at a time
Fit	Zoom Control	Lets you change the displayed magnification or fit the page to the screen
Close	Close	Closes the Preview window, not the database
	Office Links	Lets you use the table for a Word Mail Merge or insert into an Excel table
	Database Window	Switches to the database window, without closing the preview
	New Object	Lets you create a new table, query, form, report, macro, or module without returning to the database window

Table 4.1 Preview Toolbar Buttons and Their Uses

SHORTCUT

You can also set the Margins and Layout options for forms and reports, and the Margins options for datasheets, by selecting Setup in the Print dialog box.

The Page Setup option will be dimmed when the Tables page of the database window is displayed. To set up a page for a table, open the table first. The box will not contain a Layout page.

CHANGING PAGE LAYOUT

If you do not like how your printout appears in preview, then you're not going to like how it prints. Most printout problems are caused by the page layout—the margins, page size, or other settings. So before printing, or even after if you have to print it over, set the page layout how you want it.

Each object in the database, that is, each form, report, and datasheet, can have its own page layout settings. You can use one set of margins for one report and a different set for another. Either open the object you want to set the layout for, or click on its name in the database window. Then choose Page Setup from the File menu.

The Page Setup dialog box has three pages—Margins, Layout, and Page—as shown in Figure 4.4. The Margins page lets you change the page margins and whether you want to print just the data from the form, or the data, labels, and any other text or graphics. The options on the Layout page, shown in Figure 4.5, control the layout of forms or report sections.

Grid Settings controls how many forms print across the page, if more than one can fit, and their spacing. Item Size sets the size of the

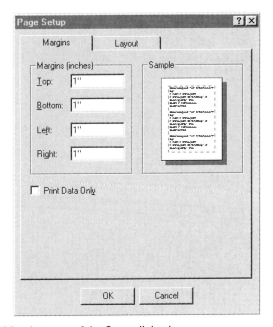

Figure 4.4 Margins page of the Setup dialog box

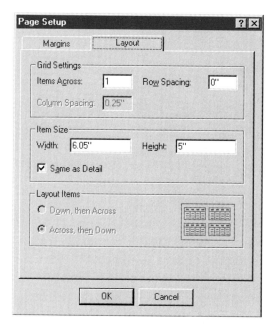

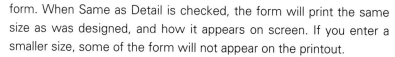

Figure 4.5 Layout page of the Setup dialog box

form. When Same as Detail is checked, the form will print the same size as was designed, and how it appears on screen. If you enter a smaller size, some of the form will not appear on the printout.

Layout Items determines the order of the forms and report sections. If you select Down, then Across, Access first fits as many records as it can down the left side of the page, then continues with more records to their right. When you select Across, then Down, Access fits as many across the top of the page, and then continues in rows below them.

In the Page section of the dialog box, you select the orientation, the page size, and source, and you set a printer to be used for the current object. The settings in the Page Setup dialog box affect just the selected object in the database window, and they are saved along with the database.

PRINTING FORMS, REPORTS, AND DATASHEETS

Viewing information on the screen is nice, but if you don't have a laptop does it mean you have to lug around your desktop? Talk about

habits & strategies

While you do not have to open a table or form to print it, it takes just a few seconds to open it and confirm it is really the object you want to print.

Still the wrong printer? Click on the Start button in the Windows 95 Taskbar, point to Settings, and click on Printers. Then use the Add Print program to install and set up your printer. You'll need your original setup disk or CD.

exercise. Fortunately, anything on the Access screen can also be printed—forms, datasheets, and reports.

Printing is a snap. First, either select the object you want to print (form, table, or report) in the database window, open the object, or display it in preview. Then just click on the Print button in the toolbar (shown here). Access will send all of the information to your printer.

If you want to print specific records or pages or otherwise control the printing process, then select Print from the File menu or press CTRL-P. Access will display the dialog box shown in Figure 4.6. This dialog box is pretty much straightforward Windows stuff.

The Printer section of the Print dialog box shows which printer will be used. Wrong printer? Pull down the Name list and select the correct one. Click the Properties button to fine-tune the printer setup, and use the Print to File option to output the print job to a file on your disk that you can print later or E-Mail.

The Print Range section of the Print dialog box determines how many records will print. All prints them all. Pages prints just those pages designated in the From and To boxes. Selected Record(s) prints just the selected records.

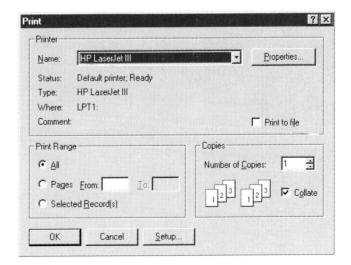

Figure 4.6 Print dialog box

The Copies section determines...well, you know. Collate is useful when printing more than one copy. When selected, each complete set of forms prints separately. When not selected, you get multiple copies of the first page, then multiple copies of the second page, and so on.

When everything is set the way you want it, click on OK.

SO WHAT'S NEXT?

Put the pink sofa over there, and then move the chair to the other side of the fireplace. No, maybe on the other side. We all like to decorate and customize our surroundings to make things just more livable. It's no different with Access. In Chapter 5, you'll learn how to customize the way Access works so that it works the way you like it.

Stuff You Only Have to Do Once to Make Your Life Easier

INCLUDES

- Setting Access options

- Moving and displaying toolbars

- Creating custom toolbars

FAST FORWARD

SET ACCESS OPTIONS ➤ pp 90-94
1. Open a database.
2. Choose Options from the Tools menu.
3. Click on each tab and select options.
4. Close the dialog box.

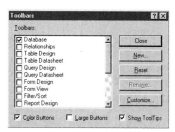

MOVE A TOOLBAR ➤ p 95
- Point to the blank area around any button and drag the toolbar.

DISPLAY/HIDE TOOLBARS ➤ pp 95-96
Open the object that displays the toolbar, or follow these steps:
1. Right-click on a toolbar.
2. Click on Toolbars.
3. Click on the check box for the toolbar you want to display or hide.
4. Close the dialog box.

ADD BUTTONS TO A TOOLBAR ➤ pp 96-97
1. Display the toolbar.
2. Right-click on the toolbar.
3. Click on Customize.
4. Select the category of the function you want to perform.
5. Drag the button to its position in the toolbar.
6. Close the dialog box.

CREATE A NEW TOOLBAR ➤ *pp 96-98*

1. Right-click on a toolbar.
2. Click on Toolbars.
3. Click on New.
4. Type the toolbar name and select OK.
5. Click on Customize.
6. Add the buttons to the toolbar.
7. Close the dialog box.

Default settings are great, if they give you what you want and need. If not, why suffer the capriciousness of Microsoft? You can change things so Access looks and works the way you want it to. In fact, you can change many of the default settings, even create custom toolbars, and then go on your merry way without even thinking about it again. How badly can you screw things up? Not at all. You can always change the settings back again.

SETTING DATABASE OPTIONS

Access lets you change a number of default settings to customize it for the way you like to work. The command you use is called Options, which is appropriate because the choices are up to you. You can leave everything set as it is, or you can pick and choose which settings you want to change. Microsoft gives us nine pages of options that we can change, a lot of which are for really advanced users, people who administer networks or workgroups, and those who love to live on the edge. However, there are other options that may really help you work with Access. We'll just mention a few that we think you might want to consider.

Open any of your databases—the Options command will be dimmed in the Tools menu when you do not have a database open. Choose Options from the Tools menu to see the dialog box shown with the View tab displayed in Figure 5.1.

The options in the Tables/Queries, Forms/Reports, Module, and Advanced pages are used for special purposes. They won't make a lot of sense to you until you learn how to create your own tables, queries, and other objects, so we won't waste your time with them now. For example, options on the Tables/Queries page determine the default settings of tables and queries. You can change these values in the table or query you create, or you can change them for every new table or query by using this dialog box. They'll mean something to you after you read Chapter 6, so come back and visit these options later.

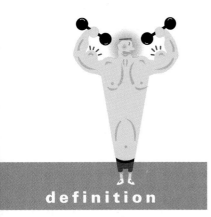

definition

Options: *Settings that Microsoft has determined we can be trusted to change.*

Figure 5.1 The View page of the Options dialog box

Glance over these other pages on your screen, and file these options away in your gray matter until later.

Changing What's Displayed on the Screen

You might find a couple of options interesting in the View page of the dialog box. For example, you can turn off the display of the status bar, if you don't find it useful and you want to squeeze one more datasheet row onto the screen. The status bar is not all that useful in Access, so you probably won't notice if it's gone.

If you have trouble seeing the toolbar buttons, select the Large Toolbar Buttons option. The buttons will be about twice the size. Of course, this means that with some toolbars you'll no longer see all of the buttons across the screen, but you can move the toolbars (as you'll learn later in this chapter). You can also change to black and white buttons, which might help on some laptops with cheapo displays, and you can turn off the display of ToolTips, if you like working on a tightrope without a net.

Customizing the Default Layout

Click on the General tab (see Figure 5.2). If you don't like the default one-inch margins for printing forms, reports, and datasheets,

enter new margins here. Your settings affect all new forms and reports and all existing datasheets. To change the margins of an existing form and report, you need to select it and use the Page Setup dialog box.

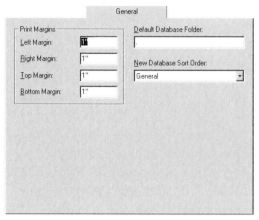

Figure 5.2 General options

Streamlining Find and Replace

Now look at the Edit/Find page (see Figure 5.3). The Default Find/Replace options determine the default settings in the Find and Replace dialog boxes. You can change any of the settings once you display the Find or Replace dialog box, but this is how they'll start:

- Fast Search searches just the current field and matches on the whole field. Looking for Smith, for example, will not match with Asmithson.
- General Search looks through every field and finds a match regardless of where the characters are located. So, a search for Smith will match the characters in Asmithson.
- Start of Field Search matches the beginning characters of the current field. It will find a match with Smithson, but not with Asmithson.

The Confirm options determine if a warning box will appear asking you to confirm certain actions. We advise leaving them selected, to play it safe (unless you want to play a dirty trick on some unsuspecting user).

CAUTION

Really think twice before you turn off the Confirm options.

Figure 5.3 Edit/Find options

Please see Chapter 3 if the Font and Cells Effects boxes have slipped your mind (we won't be insulted).

Customizing Your Datasheets

The Datasheet page lets you set the default appearance for datasheets. It offers the same choices as the Font and Cells Effects dialog boxes (that's why we're not even showing it to you here) as well as the chance to set the default column width. Use this box if you have a special combination of effects that you want to use for every datasheet.

Streamlining Keyboard Entry

The Keyboard page (see Figure 5.4) can be your best friend if you use the TAB, ENTER, or arrow keys to move around the datasheet or form. So take your time and consider these options carefully.

The options in the Move After Enter section determine what happens when you press the ENTER key. You can select to have Access stay where it is, move to the next field, or move to the next record. The default setting is Next Field, so after you enter information into a field, you just press ENTER to move to the next field, or from the last field on to the next record.

The Arrow Key Behavior options determine what happens when you press the arrow keys when a field is selected. Normally, when a field is selected, pressing an arrow key moves to the next field in the direction of the arrow. If you change the setting to Next Character, pressing an arrow key unselects the field and remains there so you can edit the contents.

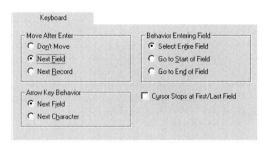

Figure 5.4 Keyboard options

The Behavior Entering Field options determine what happens when you press TAB or ENTER to move to a field. The default is Select Entire Field. If you want to go to a field and then start editing immediately, you can change this to either Go to Start of Field or Go to End of Field. When you move into a field, the insertion point will move to that position so you can start typing or editing.

Finally, the Cursor Stops at First/Last Field option determines what happens when you reach the first or the last field. When this option is not selected, pressing the RIGHT ARROW key when the last field is selected will move to the next record, or the previous record when you press the LEFT ARROW key from the first field. If you select this option, Access won't move off the field to the next record.

AH! THE WONDER OF TOOLBARS

You've already used many of the buttons in the toolbar, and you might have also displayed the Formatting (Datasheet) toolbar in Chapter 3. You also know that the toolbar will change when you do certain functions. The toolbar shown when you're looking at the database window, for example, is not the same when looking at a form or previewing an object.

Access has 19 different toolbars—that's a lot of buttons, many of which most of us will never get to use. We've talked about a lot of them throughout the first several chapters in this book, and we'll cover many more as we continue. However, Microsoft's standard selections may not match your personal needs as closely as they should. In this section, we'll offer some suggestions for keeping the most handy buttons within reach.

Making Toolbars Handier

The toolbars appear across the top of the window beneath the menu bar. If you think a toolbar will be more convenient somewhere else, then you can move it by dragging. Access will remember the position of the toolbar when you exit, so the toolbar will be in the same position the next time it is displayed.

To move a toolbar, point to a blank area around any of the buttons and then drag the toolbar to a new position. As you drag, an outline of the bar moves with the mouse, showing the position and size it will be when you release the button. If you drag the toolbar to the left or right edge of the Access window, it will be vertical with all of its buttons in a column. If you drag it to the bottom of the window, or back under the menu bar, all of the buttons will be in one row. Move the toolbar anywhere else so it appears in a window, like this:

When the toolbar appears as a window, you can drag one of its borders to change the size, or click on its Close box to remove it from the screen.

Displaying the toolbar as a window is particularly useful if you've selected to display large buttons in the Options dialog box. This way, you'll see all of the buttons.

Displaying Other Toolbars

Access usually displays the appropriate toolbar for the object on the screen. Other toolbars are optional, such as the Formatting (Datasheet) toolbar. To see if Access recommends an optional toolbar, point to any toolbar and click the right mouse button. Any optional

toolbars will be listed below the name of the default toolbar—click on one to display it.

You can also manually display additional toolbars. In most cases, however, another toolbar will only duplicate buttons in the toolbar already shown, or its buttons will be dimmed because they cannot be used with the current object. For example, if you display the Formatting (Datasheet) toolbar when a datasheet is not on screen, the buttons will be dimmed and the text boxes will be empty. A pretty useless toolbar in that condition. About the only generally useful toolbar is the Microsoft toolbar, which has buttons for quickly running or switching to other Microsoft applications.

To display another toolbar, right-click on a toolbar and select Toolbars from the shortcut menu to see this dialog box:

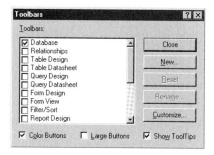

The check boxes of the toolbars already displayed will be checked. To display another toolbar, click on its check box. The toolbar appears as soon as you click, so you do not have to exit the dialog box. Deselect the box to remove the toolbar from the screen. If you turn off all of the toolbars by mistake, you can't right-click to display the shortcut menu, so use the Toolbars option from the View menu to see the Toolbars dialog box, and then click to select the proper toolbar.

The Toolbars dialog box also lets you select large buttons, color buttons, and ToolTips.

Creating Custom Toolbars

Microsoft has done a good job in designing the toolbars, but even Microsoft isn't perfect. For example, you may find yourself changing the page layout frequently, sometimes adjusting margins, page orientation, or grid settings until you like the preview or until you get a printout that you like. In this case, you may get tired of opening the File menu and selecting Page Setup each time. Another example is opening the

Find dialog box to repeat a search for the same text after closing the box prematurely. You can add buttons for these functions to your own toolbar. The Page Setup and Find Next buttons look like this:

Find Next ————————→  ←———————— Page Setup

Luckily, Access lets us modify the toolbars by adding other buttons to them. First, make sure that the toolbar you want to add a button to is displayed on the screen. Either use the Toolbars dialog box, or use other means to display the toolbar: if you want to add a button to the Form View toolbar, for example, open any form.

Next, right-click on any toolbar and choose Customize from the shortcut menu to see the dialog box shown in Figure 5.5. (You can also select Customize from the Toolbars dialog box.) In the Categories list are all of the classifications of Access functions. When you select a category, buttons for performing those functions are shown in the Buttons panel. Most of the buttons aren't very intuitive, so point to a button to see its ToolTip and a short description in the Description panel. Continue changing categories and pointing to buttons until you see the button for the function that you want. If you have to, drag the dialog box so you can see the position on the toolbar where you want to insert the button. Point to the button and drag it to that position on the toolbar. When you release the mouse, the button's in place.

As an example, we'll add a Find Next button to the Table Data-sheet toolbar, which is the toolbar that appears when you open a table

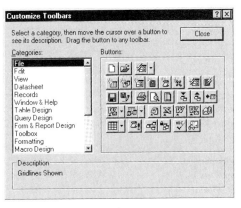

Figure 5.5 Customize Toolbars dialog box

in Datasheet View. This way, you can close the Find dialog box, and then repeat the last find by clicking the Find Next button. Just follow along.

1. Open the Contacts table so you see the toolbar.
2. Right-click on the toolbar and choose Customize.
3. If necessary, drag the dialog box down out of the way so you can see the empty area following the Delete Record button.
4. The function you want to add to the toolbar is an editing function, so click on Edit in the categories list.
5. The button you want (Find Next) is the third button from the right in the bottom row of buttons. Point to the button and drag it to the blank space following the Delete Record button.
6. Release the mouse, and then close the dialog box.

That's all there is to it. The next time you search for something in a datasheet, click on the Find button, enter the Find What text and select the search options, and click on Find Next in the dialog box. You can then close the dialog box and continue the search using the Find Next button that you've added to the toolbar.

To remove a button from a toolbar, display the Customize dialog box, and then drag the button off of the toolbar. When you release the mouse, the button will be gone. If you mess up one of the default toolbars, such as deleting or adding buttons by mistake, display the Toolbars dialog box, click on the name of the toolbar, and then click on Reset.

You use the New button in the Toolbars dialog box to create your very own toolbar. Click on New, and then enter a name for the toolbar in the dialog box that appears. A small blank toolbar will appear on screen. Use the Customize box to add buttons to it. If you decide to later delete the entire toolbar, click on its name (not its check box) in the Toolbars dialog box. The Reset command button will be labeled Delete. Click on Delete to remove the toolbar.

SO WHAT'S NEXT?

It's time to move on, away from the security of Almost Instant Databases. In the next chapter, we'll show you how to create your own databases and tables and how to modify tables once you create them. Heavy stuff.

The toolbar in Datasheet View has the same default buttons as the toolbar in Form View, but the two toolbars are not actually the same. If you display a form, your Find Next button will not appear. To add the button, repeat the procedure when a form is displayed.

Use the Rename option in the Toolbars dialog box to change the name of the selected toolbar.

Part 2

DOING IT YOUR WAY

CHAPTER

6

Creating a Custom Database and Tables

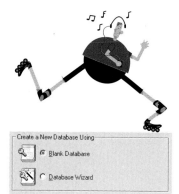

FAST FORWARD

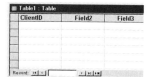

CREATE A DATABASE ➤ *pp 105-106*

1. Select Blank Database from the Startup dialog box, or click on the New Database button and double-click on Blank Database.
2. Type the database name.
3. Click on OK.

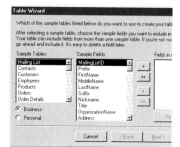

CREATE A TABLE IN DATASHEET VIEW ➤ *pp 106-108*

1. Display the Tables page of the database window.
2. Click on New.
3. Select Datasheet View.
4. Click on OK.
5. Double-click on column labels and enter field names.
6. Enter information in rows of the datasheet.
7. Click on the Save button.
8. Enter the table name and click on OK.

USE TABLE WIZARD ➤ *pp 108-112*

1. Display the Tables page of the database window.
2. Click on New.
3. Select Table Wizard.
4. Click on OK.
5. Complete the Wizard dialog boxes as they appear.

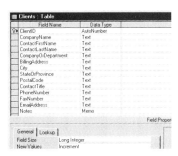

CREATE A TABLE IN DESIGN VIEW ➤ *pp 112-115*

1. Display the Tables page of the database window.
2. Click on New.
3. Select Design View.
4. Click on OK.
5. Enter the field name.
6. Select the field type.
7. Set field properties.
8. Repeat for each additional field.
9. Click on the Save button.
10. Enter a table name and select OK.

MODIFY A TABLE ➤ *pp 126-127*

1. Display the Tables page of the database window.
2. Click on the table.
3. Click on Design.
4. Add, delete, or modify the fields.
5. Click on the Save button.

Almost Instant Databases are great, but they certainly don't do everything you'd need a database for. You may want special fields that Microsoft never even thought of giving you, or you might want a combination of properties for controlling what the user can input. Sure, you could probably live with the Almost Instant Databases, but you can also get mucho frustrated trying to fit your information into someone else's database design. That's when you have to create your own database and tables, or at least change those created by the Database Wizard.

GET READY TO RUMBLE

First, a little preamble to explain the rules of the game.

If you wanted to record some simple information about your stamp collection, all you might need is a single table. Of course, you can't have a table without a database to store it in. Rather than create a separate database for your table, you could add the table to one of your existing databases. So, for example, you could store your stamp collection table in the Contacts database, or in any other database.

You could do this, but it's not ideal. In theory, if there are several tables in a database, they should all relate to the same general theme—your business, your household accounts, your Edward D. Wood, Jr. fan club, or the like. They should never be mixed. The gurus will tell you never to put a table about something personal in your business database, or add a stamp collection table to your bowling league database. That's the ideal, and it is a nice goal.

But, in reality, you can have any number of unrelated tables in the same database. So you could have one database holding your household inventory, your membership records, your bowling scores, or whatever. If that's how you want to do it, go ahead. We don't always have to live by the rules, do we? All you have to remember is that everything in this chapter about creating a table can be applied to any database. If we show you how to add a table to a business database, you can use the same techniques to add any table to any database.

For you busy people out there, we'll show you how to create a database and tables with as little work as possible. Then we'll show you how to design a database when you need something special and when you have the time. Now let's boogie.

CREATING A DATABASE

Creating a database is about the easiest thing you can do with Access. When you start Access, select Blank Database from the Startup dialog box. If you select Database Wizard by mistake, select the Blank Database template. The File New Database dialog box will appear. Access suggests the name db1 (or db2, and so on). Since that doesn't tell you much about what the database is used for (or say much for Microsoft's imagination), type your own database name and then click on Create. Access will display the database window for your new database. Couldn't be any quicker, so create your own database now, naming it My Company.

CREATING TABLES

A database won't do you much good without a table. There are a lot of ways to create a table, and it all depends on how much work you want to do and how fancy you want the table to be. In the database window, make sure the Tables page is displayed and then click on New to see this dialog box:

If you're already in Access, select New Database from the File menu or click on the New Database button in the toolbar. You'll see the list of templates to select. Double-click on the Blank Database option.

SHORTCUT

You can create a table without returning to the database window. Pull down the New Object button in a toolbar and select New Table.

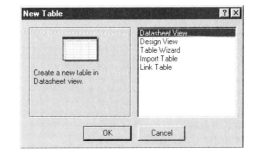

Access gives you five ways to create a table. The Import Table Wizard and Link Table Wizard let you create an Access table from a database you've already created using some other database program. We'll show you how to use these options in Chapter 11. The other three options can be classified as the following:

- Datasheet View for a quick and basic table.
- Table Wizard for a quick and elegant table.
- Design View for any type of not-so-quick table.

upgrade note

If you're familiar with creating tables manually in previous versions of Access, then you'll love Datasheet View. It's the easiest way to create a table and start entering information in one step.

CREATING A QUICK AND BASIC DATASHEET TABLE

Datasheet View is new to this version of Access, and it's a great way to create a simple table when you need to enter information right away. You create a table by naming the fields and entering data. Nothing fancy or elegant, it's just fast and convenient. You won't be able to catalog the Library of Congress by creating tables in this view, but you can't beat it for speed and ease when all you need is a simple table. Anyway, you can always modify the table later in Design View to add all of the bells and whistles.

In fact, let's create an inventory table now.

1. Click on New in the Tables page of the database window.
2. Click on Datasheet View and then select OK. A blank datasheet with 20 columns appears, with the columns labeled Field1, Field2, and so on.
3. Double-click on Field1 (or select Rename Column from the shortcut menu when you right-click on it).
4. The text in the field will be selected, so type **Item** and then press ENTER.

CAUTION

You can use the same technique to rename a field. However, don't try that yet in your Almost Instant Databases. Access would not be able to use the field in existing forms and reports.

CAUTION

Do not use the field name ID if you want Access to create a primary key for you.

CAUTION

If you do not enter data into at least one record, Access will define each field as text. You'll learn all about field types later on.

5. Double-click on Field2, and type **Quantity**. You cannot use ENTER, TAB, or the arrow keys to move from one field name to another; you must double-click on the field name cell.

6. In the same way as in step 5, rename Field3 as Cost, Field4 as Expires, and Field5 as VendorID.

Now enter some information into the datasheet. Access is going to know the type of field by the information that you enter, so be consistent. In the Quantity and Cost fields, for example, always enter numbers. In the Expires field, always enter a date. Complete the datasheet so it looks like this:

	Item	Quantity	Cost	Expires	VendorID
▶	Jelly, Cherry	76	4.5	3/6/97	105
	Jelly, Grape	34	3.75	2/16/97	105
	Cider, Apple	102	2.15	11/3/97	102
	Coffee Beans	56	5.76	10/3/97	103
	Jelly, Orange	46	4.26	1/4/97	101
	Cider, Grape	97	2.79	10/1/97	102
	Apricots, dried	56	7.76	5/3/97	104
	Bananas, dried	87	6.57	6/5/97	104
	Cider, Cherry	78	3.45	8/14/97	102
	Figs, dried	56	8.98	4/16/97	104
	Jelly, Lime	12	3.14	9/23/97	101
	Peaches, dried	68	10.87	7/3/97	104
*					

Click on the Save button, shown here, to display the Save As dialog box. Access will imaginatively suggest the name Table1 (if it's the first table you have created so far). We can do better, so type **Inventory** and then click on OK.

A dialog box appears warning you that you do not have a primary key. A primary key is not absolutely necessary for a quick and dirty table like this, so you *could* select No and go on your merry way. But primary keys make things a lot easier, so click on Yes now to see what Access does. The table appears on the screen with an AutoNumber field as the first column. Although the field name cell appears blank, Access did indeed name the field ID. Let's name it something else. Double-click on the blank cell and type **ItemID**.

You're done. The table is created, so close the table to return to the database window.

CREATING A QUICK AND ELEGANT TABLE

So much for quick and basic. Now let's look at quick and elegant using the Table Wizard. Table Wizard is to tables what Database Wizard is to databases. It will create a complete table for you, letting you select from various purposes and fields. Instead of trying to decide what fields you'll need to create, you can let Access create them for you.

The Tables page of the database window should be displayed, so click on New, choose Table Wizard, and then click on OK. You'll see the first Wizard dialog box (Figure 6.1). The list on the left shows some sample tables. Under the list are the option buttons Business and Personal. The option selected determines the types of tables listed. Click on Personal to see suggested tables for personal pursuits. Click on Business for typical business tables.

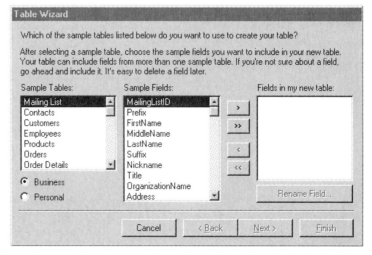

Figure 6.1 Selecting the type of table, the table itself, and then the fields

Now scroll the Sample Tables list to see the types of tables available. When you select a table, suggested fields appear in the list box in the center. Click on Customers, because you're going to create a clients table for your company database.

The trick now is to move the fields you want to use from the list box in the center into the list box on the right. To move an individual field, click on its name in the list and then on the > button. If you want to use all or almost all of the fields, just click on the >> button—you can then remove the individual fields that you do not want. We want all of the fields except one, so click on the >> button. Now remove the Country field by clicking on it in the list box on the right—you'll have to scroll to reach it—then click on the < button.

Next, rename the CustomerID field to ClientID (client sounds more professional than customer). Click on CustomerID and then on the Rename Field button. Type **ClientID** in the dialog box that appears, and then click on OK.

When the list box on the right contains all of the fields that you want, click on Next to see the dialog box shown in Figure 6.2. Here you give the table a name and choose if you want Access to set the primary key for you. Type **Clients** as the table name, and click on Next to let Access name the primary key for you. Access will select an appropriate field—in this case, ClientID—as the field and assign it an AutoNumber type.

You'll now see the dialog box in Figure 6.3. This box only appears when tables already exist in the database. If a table has a field that matches the primary key of your new table, Access will suggest a relationship. You can accept Access's choice, remove the relationship, or create a new one on your own. We'll look at relationships in Chapter 7, so just click on Next.

The final Wizard dialog box appears with three options:

- Modify the Table Design opens the table in Design View. You use this view to change the table, add fields, change the field types, or change the way the field accepts data.

habits & strategies

You can mix and match fields from any number of tables. Move the field from one table into the list box on the right, then choose another table from either category (Business or Personal), and select additional fields as you want.

- Enter Data Directly Into The Table just opens the table in Datasheet View.
- Enter Data Directly Into The Table Using A Form The Wizard Creates For Me (probably the longest option name in history) will create a form and display it on the screen for entering information. This is a great option to select, because it saves you the trouble of creating a form later on—although it only takes two or three clicks to do it anyway.

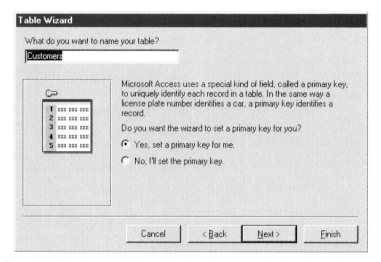

Figure 6.2 Naming your table and having Access assign it a primary key

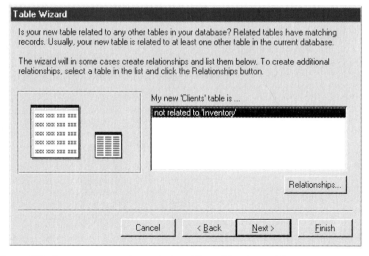

Figure 6.3 Access suggesting relationships with other tables

For now, select Enter Data Directly Into The Table and click on Finish. Your table will appear as shown below.

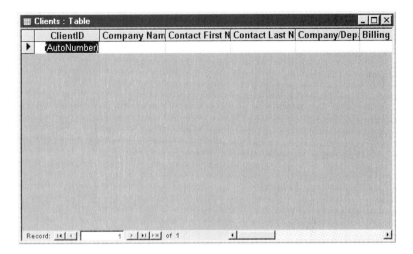

Enter the information shown in Figure 6.4 into the table, making up your own data for the columns that aren't shown in the figure, and then close the table to return to the database window.

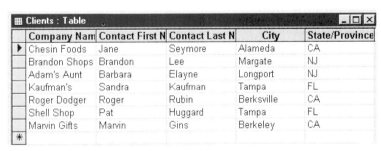

Company Nam	Contact First N	Contact Last N	City	State/Province
Chesin Foods	Jane	Seymore	Alameda	CA
Brandon Shops	Brandon	Lee	Margate	NJ
Adam's Aunt	Barbara	Elayne	Longport	NJ
Kaufman's	Sandra	Kaufman	Tampa	FL
Roger Dodger	Roger	Rubin	Berksville	CA
Shell Shop	Pat	Huggard	Tampa	FL
Marvin Gifts	Marvin	Gins	Berkeley	CA

Figure 6.4 Information to enter into the table

Modifying Tables in Datasheet View

Before we delve into the inner sanctum of tables in Design View, you should know that you can rename, add, and delete fields directly in its datasheet. You can modify any table in Datasheet View, no matter how it was created.

To rename a field, double-click on its field name and type a new name. You can also point to the field name so the mouse pointer appears as a black down arrow. Then click the right mouse button and choose Rename Column from this shortcut menu:

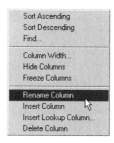

To delete a field, right-click on the field name and choose Delete Column from the shortcut menu. A box appears warning you that deleting the column will permanently delete the field and the information in it. Select Yes only if you are sure.

To add a field to the datasheet, and thus to the table, right-click on the field name that you want to follow your new field. Then choose Insert Column from the shortcut menu. A new column will be added labeled Field1 or the next highest field number. Change the name and enter data.

You'll learn how to use the Insert Lookup Column option in Chapter 7.

DESIGNING A TABLE

Finally we come to creating a table in Design View. Now we know you're busy, but if you want to have complete control over your table for a really professional database, then you'll find this useful. Creating a table in Design View is not for the fainthearted or for those who are really busy and find that Table Wizard fits all of their needs. It's good to learn about Design View, however, even if you do use the Wizard or Datasheet View, because Design View includes methods you use to change a table that cannot be done using Datasheet View. All of the techniques that you'll learn here, in fact, can be applied to making a table as well as modifying one.

In Design View, you not only type the names of fields, but you must select their types and you have the opportunity to set their properties. The type tells Access what kind of entries are allowed in the field. Properties determine how you can enter information into a field,

how it appears on screen, and how it is stored with the database. There are three steps to creating a field:

1. Enter the field name.
2. Select its type.
3. (Option) Set its properties.

To create a table in Design View, select Design View from the New Table dialog box and then click on OK. You'll see the Design View window shown in Figure 6.5.

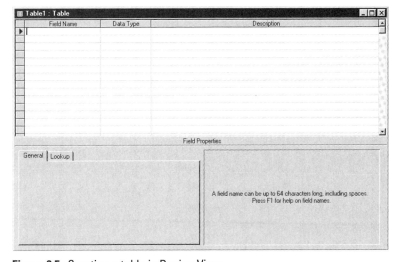

Figure 6.5 Creating a table in Design View

There are three columns in the top of the window. In the column on the left, you enter the name of the field. In the second column, you select the field type. In the third column, you enter an optional description. Many gurus will tell you that the description is important, but a lot of people don't bother with them.

Now there's a lot to explain about Design View, especially if you want to take advantage of field properties. This means that we'll have to interrupt the nice flow of instructions with some explanations. Don't get hung up on the details. If it's something you don't think you'll need, just scan the material and go on. You can always return to Design View to modify your table later on. Once you get the basics down pat, you can concentrate on the subtleties of field properties, OK? Let's continue.

You move around the Design View screen just as you do with a datasheet. Click where you want to enter information or use the TAB, SHIFT-TAB, ENTER, and arrow keys.

Creating a Field to Number Records

The AutoNumber field is convenient, because it will number your records for you. Use it for client numbers or another field that must be unique for each record. You're only allowed one AutoNumber field in a table, so pick it wisely.

1. In the first blank cell under Field Name, in the top row, type **OrderNumber**.
2. Press TAB to reach the Data Type column. The down arrow appears, indicating a pull-down list.
3. Click on the arrow to see the field types, and select AutoNumber. (You see, not every AutoNumber field must end with the letters ID.)

Understanding Field Types

Before going on to the next field, here are the nine types of fields that you can create.

- Text: Use for any field that won't be used for performing calculations and that doesn't fit into any of these other categories; entries can be up to 255 characters.
- Memo: Use when you'll need to type more than 255 characters, sort of a mini word processor for up to 64,000 characters in the field.
- Number: Use only when you'll need to perform math and when you don't need it formatted as currency.
- Date/Time: Obviously, use only when you need to enter dates and times; by specifying this type, you can perform math on dates, such as calculating the number of days between two dates.
- Currency: Same as number but with a fixed number of decimal places and a dollar sign (if you're using the American version of Access, that is).
- AutoNumber: Use when you want Access to automatically number the record for you. In previous versions of Access, this was called the Counter type.
- Yes/No: Use only when a field can be either a yes or no value, such as Paid?, High School Graduate?, or Passed

Inspection? The field will appear with a check box. Checked means Yes; unchecked means No.

- OLE: Use for pictures, sound files, or graphs.
- Lookup Wizard: Use to create a field that lets you select a value from a field in another table. This isn't really a field type—so you have to select the field type first—but a way to enter information into the table.

INVESTING IN PROPERTY

We accepted all of the default properties for the first field. In general, if you don't have to change something, just leave it, but there are times when you'll want to set special properties. For example, suppose you want to control how you can enter the date into a table or form and how it should appear on the screen. Or, perhaps you want Access to enter the date automatically to make it easier to complete a record. That's when you need to set the field's properties.

1. In the second row under Field Name, type **Date**.
2. Press TAB to reach the Data Type column.
3. Pull down the list and click on Date/Time.
4. Click in the Format text box in the Field Properties pane at the bottom of the window.
5. Pull down the list to see the type of date and time formats allowed.
6. Click on Short Date. This determines how the date appears *after* you've entered it.
7. Click on the Input Mask text box, and type **99/99/00**. This determines the way you must enter the date. The number 9 means that you can enter either a digit or space in that position but that it is not required.
8. Click on the Caption text box and type **Order Date**. Order Date will appear in the datasheet and when you create forms and reports, rather than the name of the field. You can still use the shorter field name in expressions and calculations.
9. Click in the Default Value box and enter **=Date()**. This function inserts the current date for you automatically for all new records.

Now let's see what you just did and look at some field properties in detail. (If you don't care, please scan through the section anyway.)

Customizing a Field with Properties

Properties determine how a field is entered, displayed, and stored. The properties shown in the window depend on the type of field. Some properties will have default values, while others will be blank. If you don't want to bother about the properties, you can just go on, but properties do give you greater control over your database and they ensure that your information is valid. Here's a summary of the properties used by Access. Just remember that not all of these properties will appear for each field type.

- Field Size: For text and number fields. With text fields, set the number of characters from 1 to 255 (the default is 50). For number fields, select Byte, Integer, Long Integer, Single, Double, or Replication ID.
- Byte: Can only accept a number from 0 to 255.
- Integer and Long Integer: Numbers without decimal places. Integers can be between negative and positive 32,768; long integers between negative and positive 2 billion.
- Single and Double: Numbers with decimals. Single to 38 places; double to 308.
- Replication ID: Used for primary key fields with tables in briefcases. A briefcase lets you synchronize files to maintain up-to-date copies (replicas) between computers, such as your desktop and laptop.
- Format: Determines how the information appears on screen and when printed. With text fields, for example, the most common entry is >, which converts all lowercase characters to uppercase, such as for state abbreviations.
- Decimal Places: The number of decimal places for number and currency fields.
- New Values: For AutoNumber fields, select either increment (1, 2, 3...) or random (who knows?).
- Input Mask: Specifies the format in which information is entered.

- Caption: A more descriptive name for the field to be used in forms and reports. Use a caption when you enter a short field name to fit in a datasheet column and to conform to other database naming conventions.
- Default Value: Information that will appear in the field automatically, but that you can change in the datasheet or form. The entry =Date() is a special function that tells Access to insert the current date. If all of your clients are in California, enter CA as the default value in the property for the State field.
- Validation Rule: A logical expression that determines whether Access accepts your field entry.
- Validation Text: A message that appears if information violates the validation rule.
- Required: Determines if an entry must be made in the field.
- Allow Zero Length: This is too complicated to explain here; see our explanation later in the chapter.
- Indexed: Determines if an index will be created to provide faster searches. You'll learn more about indexes later in this chapter and in Chapter 7.

Input Mask

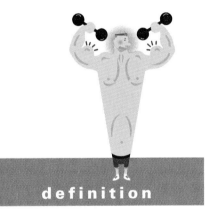

definition

Input mask: A series of special characters that establish the pattern for your entries.

Short and simple, input masks do two important things. They save you the trouble of entering certain characters, like the parentheses and hyphens in the phone number, and they ensure that even the most careless person can't screw up your database. Sure, you can set up rules, write procedures, and train staff. But it doesn't mean that everyone follows the rules or pays attention during the training session.

Here's an example. For some reason, companies come up with the weirdest conventions for inventory stock numbers. So suppose your company decides to assign an inventory code that starts with the letters XY (the initials of the owner's wife) followed by five numbers. We can just bet that sometime, somehow, someone will forget the rule. Or to give the benefit of the doubt, someone may just make a typographic error.

When you want to ensure that data gets entered in the correct format, use an input mask. The mask characters are shown in Table 6.1. Any other character is a literal. For example, use (999) 000-0000 in a

Mask Character	Allowable Entries
0	Only digits 0 to 9, required
9	Optional digit or space
#	Digit or space, as well as plus and minus signs
L	Letter A to Z, required
?	Optional letter A to Z
A	Any letter or digit, required
a	Any optional letter or digit
&	Any character or a space, required
C	Any optional character or a space
.	Decimal point
,	Thousands separator
: ; - /	Date and time separators
<	All characters following will be converted to lowercase
>	All characters following will be converted to uppercase (use >LL in a state field, for example)
!	Characters will appear from right to left, rather than from left to right; only works when characters on the left are optional
\	Displays the next character, even if it is an input mask character (using \& will actually display the & character)
"Password"	Displays an asterisk for each character typed

Table 6.1 Input Mask Characters

A Format property takes precedence over an Input Mask property. For example, if the format is < (for lowercase) and the input mask is >LL (for uppercase), the text will appear as lowercase.

telephone field to display the parentheses and hyphen in the mask. For your inventory numbers, use the mask XY00000. The letters XY will appear on the screen, and the user must enter five numbers. Want a five-digit or nine-digit zip code? Use the mask 00000-9999.

In addition to the definition characters, the mask can have two optional parts, separated by semicolons.

- Part 1: By default, only characters that you type in the field are saved on the disk. All literal placeholders (such as the parentheses and hyphen in the phone number mask) appear on screen and when printed, but they are not actually saved with the table. This is good, because it saves disk space. If you follow the mask with the number 0,

however, as in *(999) 000-0000;0*, the literals will actually be saved. Use the number 1 if you want to indicate the default setting.

- Part 2: The second option determines what character indicates the spaces you fill in on the mask. By default, spaces are shown with an underline character (_), but you can designate any other. For example, the mask *00000-9999;1;** will display *****-**** in the field. To display a blank space, use two quotation marks around a space, as in " ".

Input Mask Wizard

For phone numbers, dates, zip codes, and other common types of text and date field entries, use the Input Mask Wizard button. After entering the Input Mask property text box, click on the Build button, shown here:

Now the dialog box shown in Figure 6.6 will appear. The list box shows some general types of entries and how the corresponding information appears on screen. Select the type of entry, and then test out how it

Figure 6.6 Input Mask Wizard

upgrade note

The Edit List button in the Input Mask Wizard is new. Click on the button if you want to modify the default Wizard options or to add your own input masks to the Wizard list.

will work by clicking in the Try It box.

When you select the entry type, click on Next. For all but password entries, Access will display a dialog box where you can edit the mask and select the placeholder for spaces, as shown in Figure 6.7. (For passwords, the final Wizard box appears, so just click on Finish.) Make any changes you want to the mask or placeholder, and then try it out. When you're satisfied, click on Next. For all but date fields, the final box asks if you want to store the literals with the field or not. Make your

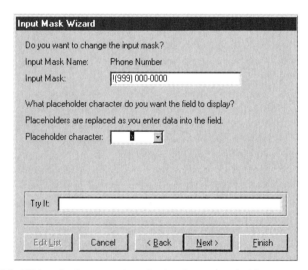

Figure 6.7 Editing the input mask and selecting a placeholder

choice and then click on Finish.

Validating Field Data

Input masks help, but your table can still fall victim to that loose cannon in the office. Your next line of defense is the validation rule. Create a text field called ShipBy and set its properties like this:

1. Set the Field Size at 5.
2. Enter > in the Format property to convert your entry to uppercase characters.
3. Set the Default Value at **UPS**.
4. Enter a Validation Rule of **IN (UPS, FEDEX, DHL, AIR, BOAT)**.
5. Enter the Validation Text of **Must be UPS, FEDEX, DHL, AIR, or BOAT**.
6. Set the Required property to Yes.

The Validation Rule property determines the valid entries that Access will accept. The rule is actually a logical expression. If your entry meets the expression criteria, then it is allowed. If the entry does not meet the criteria, then a box will appear containing the validation text when you try to move to another field. In this case, the rule uses the IN operator, which tests if your entry is one of a series of values. So, in our example, you must enter UPS, FEDEX, DHL, AIR, or BOAT. You can enter it in lowercase as well, because the format converts it to uppercase for you.

>	greater than
>=	greater than or equal to
<	less than
<=	less than or equal to
=	equal to
<>	not equal to

To test for numeric values, use any of these operators:

For example, if you're entering information in the Hourly Wage Rate field, you'd want to be sure you wouldn't enter 75.00 instead of 7.50. To avoid this problem, use a validation rule such as <10 to ensure that only rates less than $10 can be entered. To test to see if a value is within a certain range, use the BETWEEN...AND operator. An example looks like this: BETWEEN 5 AND 8.25. If the field is a date/time field, the validation rule can test for dates. You just have to surround the date with # symbols, such as >#10/22/96#, to ensure that the date entered is after October 22, 1996.

SHORTCUT

If you have just two or three options, you could also use the OR command, as in "UPS" OR "FEDEX".

Once you create a validation rule, you cannot leave the field blank, unless the ruler specifically indicates that it can be a null.

Since this will be a text field, Access will format the mask as L0\-#### to designate the hyphen is a literal and is not a date or time separator.

Text and memo fields offer even more opportunity for controlling input. You can test the entry to determine if certain characters are in specific positions, and you can limit the input to specific characters. All this is done with the LIKE operator and the wildcards ? (any single character), * (any number of characters), and # (any single number). The LIKE expression means that the input must look like a certain pattern.

This is similar to the action of an input mask but with the added advantage of a personal error message. For example, if you use an input mask to check for a valid zip code, Access will display a rather cryptic message if the user gets it wrong. Instead, use a validation rule such as LIKE "#####" OR LIKE "#####-####". This rule means that the input has to look like five numbers in a row, or five numbers followed by a hyphen and four other numbers. You can then use validation text such as "Enter either a correct 5-digit or 9-digit zip code."

To control which specific characters are allowed—something you cannot do with an input mask—enclose the valid characters in brackets. For example, suppose you use an inventory product code to identify the item's location in the warehouse. The code must start with the letter A, B, C, or D representing the section number, followed by the number 1, 2, 3, or 4 representing the bin number. These are followed by a hyphen and then up to four numbers to identify the item, such as A1-1234 to represent item 1234 in bin 1 of section A. Sounds complicated, but it's not.

Start with this input mask: L0-####. This requires a letter and a number and displays the hyphen so you don't have to type it. Then, enter the validation rule of LIKE "[ABCD][1234]####". Now only valid ID numbers can be entered—only the letters A, B, C, or D in the first position, and the numbers 1, 2, 3, or 4 in the second position.

To specify values that cannot be entered, by the way, precede them with an exclamation point. LIKE "[!XYZ]" would allow any character except X, Y, or Z.

Allow Zero Length

This is one of those strange properties that takes some extra explanation. If you do not enter anything into a record for a text or memo field, then what's there? No. This is not like "If a tree falls in the forest and no one is there, will there be any noise?"

Null is a special computer word meaning that it's blank, empty—there's nothing there. A Zero Length string is actually " ", a string with nothing in it. The two are not the same.

Is it that important a distinction? Yes. Do you have to worry about it now? No.

KEYS AND INDEXES

You can create a primary key as well as establish one or more indexes. The primary key maintains the order of the records, while the indexes help speed up searches and other operations.

To set the primary key, click on the field that you want to use for the key and then click on the Primary Key button, shown here, in the toolbar. Do that now. Click anywhere in the row for OrderNumber and then on the Primary Key button. Access places a key symbol on the field's selector bar. Notice that it also sets the Index property to Yes(No Duplicates). This means that the field will be indexed and that you cannot have the same value in more than one field. A primary key must be unique.

Let's talk about the primary key for a moment. You know that Access maintains your records in primary key order. If you sort the table using some other field, you can quickly return to the primary key order using the Remove Filer/Sort command in the Records menu.

When you use an AutoNumber field as the primary key, Access inserts the value for you and ensures that it is unique. That's why an AutoNumber field is a perfect candidate. If you use some other type of field for the primary key, then you can enter the value yourself or edit it. Not to worry. Access will ensure the value is unique by not letting you enter a duplicate value. If you enter a value that is already used as a primary key in another record, a warning box will appear, and you'll have to try again to enter a unique primary key.

In addition, you do not have to enter the records in primary key order. Suppose you use the OrderNumber field as the primary key but make it a regular number field or even a text field. You can enter the records in any order of the key value you want—OrderNumber 4, then 1, then 100, or anything. When you change views—such as from the datasheet to form—or close and then open the database, Access will automatically arrange the records in order of their primary keys.

When you end a field name with ID, Access automatically sets the Indexed property to Yes(Duplicates OK).

You'll learn more about primary keys and indexes in Chapter 7.

If you enter negative and positive values into a field when creating a table, Access applies no default format. Positive entries appear as -1, negative entries as 0. Use Design View to set the format as desired.

A combo box lets you select values from another table. You'll learn about combo boxes in Chapter 7.

Creating an Index

You can also set the index property for other fields. By indexing a field, it speeds up searches and other database operations, but it may slow down data entry somewhat.

Click on the Date field, click on the Indexed property, and then pull down the list. In addition to No, for no index, you can select Yes(Duplicates OK) and Yes(No Duplicates). Select Yes(Duplicates OK). This means that you can have the same value in more then one record. In this case, we might have any number of orders placed on the same day, which is why you select Yes(Duplicates OK). You're just indexing them to make it easier to find records by their date and produce statistical information, such as aging reports.

YES/NO FIELDS

Finally, we'll create a Yes/No type of field. In the fourth row under Field Name, type **Rush** and choose Yes/No as the data type. The Format property will appear as Yes/No. You can also select a format of True/False and On/Off. How the value actually appears in the datasheet, however, depends on a setting in the Lookup page of the properties. Click on the Lookup tab to see the option Display Control. This property will be set at Check Box. This means that a check box will appear in the field. When entering data, click in the box to indicate either an on or an off condition, just like a check box in any Windows dialog box.

You can also set the Display Control at Text Box or Combo Box. A text box will display the value as either True or False, Yes or No, or On or Off, depending on the Format property. You can enter any positive value (true, yes, on, 1, or -1) or any negative value (false, no, off, or 0). Access will convert your entries to the appropriate format. For example, if you choose the True/False format, Access will convert all other positive entries to True, and all negative entries to False.

Leave the option set at Check Box and click on the General Tab.

SETTING TABLE PROPERTIES

A field's validation rule sets criteria that must be valid before you can leave a field. You can also create a record validation rule. This is a criteria that must be valid before you can save the record or add a new one. Record validation rules generally compare the values in more than one field.

For example, suppose you don't want to ship rush orders by BOAT. You don't want to leave a record if BOAT is in the ShipBy field and the Rush field is checked.

Click on the Properties button in the toolbar or select Properties from the View menu to see this dialog box:

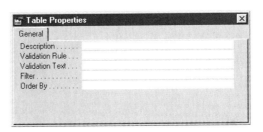

In the Validation Rule box, enter **NOT([SHIPBY]="BOAT" AND [RUSH])**. In the Validation Text box, type **Cannot ship rush delivery by boat**. The rule contains two parts combined into an AND operation. It is started by the word NOT, showing Access what is not allowed. In this case, what's not allowed is the combination of [SHIPBY]="BOAT" and [RUSH]. Since Rush is a Yes/No field, [RUSH] by itself means that it equals Yes.

Close the Table Properties dialog box. Now, you cannot have BOAT in the ShipBy field and check Rush in the same record.

The Filter and Order By properties, in the Table Properties dialog box, determine what filter and sort order will be used if you click on the Apply Filter button. If you applied a filter/sort in Datasheet View and did not clear the filter grid, you'll see the specifications in the properties. Changing these two properties will also change the specifications in the grid.

The format of the Filter property can be quite complex, as in (((City)="Orlando") AND ((StateOrProvince)="FL")). Each field name and the entire expression must be enclosed in parentheses. To specify a sort, just enter the field name in the Order By property, starting it with a minus sign to indicate a descending sort.

CAUTION

Type the validation rule exactly as shown, being careful to distinguish between the square brackets and the parentheses.

habits & strategies

The best way to learn the syntax for these properties is to create an Advanced Filter/Sort and then look at the table properties.

SAVING THE TABLE

When you are done creating your table, you must save it. Click on the Save button to save your table, and name it Orders. If you try to change to Datasheet View before saving the table, a dialog box appears telling you that you must save it first. Click on Yes to save the table and change views, or No to remain in Design View.

Then click on the Datasheet View button to see the completed table. You can close the database for now, as we'll be adding records to this table in the next chapter. Sit back and relax, and read the rest of the chapter.

Don't panic if this table doesn't seem complete. We'll be adding another field to it in Chapter 7.

MODIFYING A TABLE

All of the techniques that you've just learned can be applied to changing an existing table as well as creating a new one. Just open the table in Design View. Click on its name in the datasheet window and then select Design, or open the table and click on the first button on the left of the toolbar. You can modify a field's name, type, or properties by editing the name, selecting a new type, and choosing new properties.

To add a new field at the end of the table, just enter the field information in the first blank row. To insert a field within the table, click anywhere in the field that you want to follow the new one, and then click on the Insert Row button in the toolbar. You can also select the field by clicking in its selector bar and then pressing the INS key on the keyboard.

To delete a field, click anywhere in the field and then click on the Delete Row button. You can also select the field and then press the DEL key on the keyboard.

To reposition a field, select it and then point to its selector bar so the pointer appears like a large white arrow. Then drag the field up or down to its new position.

You can also change the field type and its properties. However, once the table has information in it, changing type or properties could produce some unwanted results. Some information may be lost, such as characters in a text field that you are changing to number. If you are creating or changing a validation rule, Access will ask if you want to check the existing information against the rule. If you select Yes, Access will report if it finds information that violates the rule, but it will not delete it. This lets you know that you should review your information to decide if you want to change it to conform to the new rule.

If you set a new primary key, Access will not be able to save the changes if any duplicates exist in the new primary key field. You'll have to remove the primary key, return to the table, and correct the duplicated information before changing the primary key.

SO WHAT'S NEXT?

Seems too easy? There's just got to be a catch? Well, yes and no. There are some more sophisticated things you'll have to know—such as creating lookup tables and relationships—to make something more than a very simple database. They're not really difficult, as you'll see in Chapter 7.

Stuff to Make the Gurus Happy

FAST FORWARD

CREATE A LOOKUP COLUMN ➤ *pp 134-138*

1. Open the table in Design View.
2. Name the field and click in the Data Type column.
3. Pull down the Data Type list and select Lookup Wizard.
4. Complete the Wizard dialog boxes as desired.

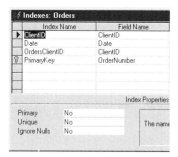

CREATE A MULTIPLE FIELD INDEX ➤ *pp 139-140*

1. Open the table in Design View.
2. Click on the Indexes button.
3. Enter the index name.
4. Select the index field.
5. Choose a sort order.
6. Set the index properties.
7. In the next blank index row, select another field and sort order.
8. Repeat step 6 for each field to be added to the index.

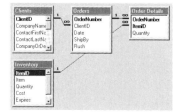

DEFINE RELATIONSHIPS ➤ *pp 140-144*

1. Open the database.
2. Click on the Relationships button.
3. If the Show Table dialog box doesn't appear, click on the Show Table button.
4. Double-click on tables to be added to the Relationships window, and then click on Close.
5. Drag between related fields.
6. Confirm fields in the Relationships dialog box.
7. If desired, select to Enforce Referential Integrity and other options.
8. Click on Create.

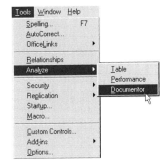

PRINT TABLE INFORMATION ➤ *pp 146-148*

1. Open the database.
2. Choose Analyze from the Tools menu.
3. Click on Documentor.
4. Select the object type, or choose All Object Types from the list.
5. Select each object you want documented, and then click on OK.
6. Read or print the report.
7. Close the report window.

You now know the basics for creating tables and data-bases. If the basics seem easy, it's because they are. If you want to move on and create a professional database—one that a guru would be proud of—you can do it slowly, in stages, and with a lot of intestinal fortitude. This chapter will get you jump-started.

DATABASE DESIGN RULES

Granted, the Database Wizard can create a complete database for you, and it's a pretty fancy database. Not only does it include tables, forms, and reports, but they are complicated ones at that—switchboards, forms with fields from multiple tables, and the like. However, if you take the trouble to learn how to design your own database, you can create even more sophisticated and useful databases. You can add to your own databases all of the powerful elements that Database Wizard provides to its own. Creating this type of database by yourself, sans wizard, isn't that difficult; it just takes quite a few steps and a little more experience.

Before you dive head first into developing all of your own data-bases and tables, you should learn a little about good database design. We know you're too busy to worry about all of the design principles that would satisfy the database guru in the office. However, it's always been our belief that if you start with just a few basic good habits, the rest will somehow find its way into your brain.

So here's our basic set of rules.

- Rule 1—Never create a field that can be calculated from other fields.

  If you have an inventory table with fields called StockOnHand and Cost, don't bother with a field containing the item's net value—the product of the two fields. For one reason, every time the amount on hand and cost change, you'd have to recalculate and edit the value in the net field. When you want to see the net value—or perform any other calculation on fields—you do so on a form or report. This way, you can see and print the results without wasting space storing them in the table. In addition, you should never design a database in which making a change on one field means that you have to make a change in another field. It's too easy to forget.

- Rule 2—Never create repeating fields.

Repeating fields are those that basically contain the same type of information. For example, suppose your club wants to keep information about member's children. How many fields do you have and what do you name them? Child1, Child2, Child3, and so on? Are we interested in family planning here, or creating a good database? You have fields that repeat the same type of information—the name of a member's child. What you need is to actually create two related tables. You'll learn about that later in this chapter.

- Rule 3—Never create a field that has the same value in every record, and which you know will be the same value.

Say that you are licensed to trade only with customers in Kentucky. Do you need a field called State? No way. All of your customers must be in Kentucky. If you're worried about printing the state name on the address, don't. You can add the state once in a form, report, or on mailing labels.

- Rule 4—Each record must be unique.

No two records should be entirely the same. If you have two records that are exactly the same, in every field, then you have done something wrong. OK, so suppose your baseball card collection has duplicates. Are they in exactly the same condition? If not, then you need a Condition field where you can record the condition of each card. If you do have exact duplicates, then you need a Duplicates or Quantity field. Don't record the same information twice, just have a field where you can indicate that you have two of the same object.

- Rule 5—You should have a primary key, and it must be unique.

A primary key helps keep your records in some type of order, and it enables you to form relationships. Enforcing a relationship's referential integrity is the best way to avoid serious errors in your database. If you do have a primary key, however, make sure that it will be unique for every record.

STREAMLINING DATA ENTRY WITH LOOKUP FIELDS

There are a lot of times when you can only enter specific values in a field. Remember the ShipBy field in the Orders table from Chapter 6? The validation rule said you could only enter FEDEX, UPS, DHL, AIR, or BOAT. Rather than trust your user to remember what to enter, create a lookup field. A lookup field displays the possible choices, so all you have to do is click on the correct one.

This is a perfect way to make a database foolproof so just about anyone can use it. For example, while taking orders over the phone, you need to record the name or ID number of the client placing the order. What would happen if, by mistake, you write down an incorrect ID number—one for a client that does not exist? When you are ready to ship the order, you won't know where to ship to and who to bill. To make sure this problem doesn't occur, you use a lookup field. When taking the order, you can just pop-down a list of client ID numbers and names. No mistakes and no problem.

The database that we've created needs a lookup table for this exact purpose, so you should add it now. Add a lookup field to the Orders table to let you pick the ClientID number from the Clients table:

habits & strategies

Use a lookup field whenever possible when information in a field must match a value in another table.

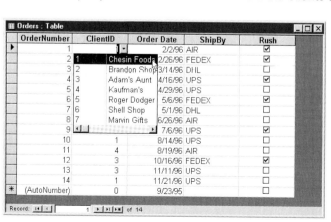

upgrade note

The Lookup Wizard is similar to the old Combo Box Wizard, but it gives you more options. You still create combo boxes and list boxes on forms and reports, however.

SHORTCUT

You can insert a lookup column directly in Datasheet View. Right-click on the field name of the column that you want to appear to the right of the lookup column, then choose Insert Lookup Column from the shortcut menu. Then complete the Wizard dialog boxes as explained here.

You have to first add a row to the table. Open the My Company database, and if necessary, click on the Tables tab. Click on the Orders table and select Design so you can add the field. Click anywhere in the row for the date field, then click on the Insert Row button to insert a blank row.

Now create the field. Type **ClientID** as the field name, pull down the Data Type list and select Number. The field type must match the corresponding field to be looked up, but while the ClientID field in the Clients table is actually an AutoNumber field, it contains numbers.

Pull down the Data Type list again and click on Lookup Wizard to see the first dialog box (Figure 7.1). This box gives you two options. The default setting will get the information for the lookup list from another table. This is what you want, so leave it set this way. The other option lets you create a list by entering the values while the Wizard is running. You would use this option, for example, if you want to list the shipping options for the ShipBy field so the user could pick from valid choices.

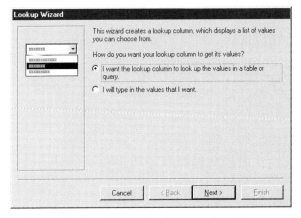

Figure 7.1 Choose to look up information from another table or to enter the choices as the Wizard is running

Click on Next to see a list of the other tables in the database. This box is really asking "Where do you want me to get the information from?" Click on the Clients table and then on Next. The third Wizard box is shown in Figure 7.2. Here you select the information that you want listed in the lookup table.

For each field you want listed, click on it and then on the > button. So click on the ClientID field and then on >. Now in the same way, add the CompanyName field to the list and then select Next. This next dialog box shows how the columns in the lookup list will appear, but only one column is shown—CompanyName. That's because the Hide the Key Column check box is selected. This is a useful option when you are creating a lookup field to use for a reference on a form. It hides the primary field so you cannot use the list to actually change information on the form. For now, deselect the box to display the ClientID column. We want the column displayed because we want to actually display the client's ID number in the Orders tables.

As the instructions say, drag the columns to adjust their width, or double-click on the right edge of a column to fit it to the heading.

Because the first column will only contain a number, double-click on the line on its right. Then click on Next to see the Wizard dialog box in Figure 7.3. This is an important one. In this dialog box, you select the field that you want inserted into the record. For example, when you select an item from the list, do you want the ClientID or Company name

Avoid selecting more than two fields. Too many fields make the lookup table bulky on the screen. Use just enough fields to identify the records to choose from.

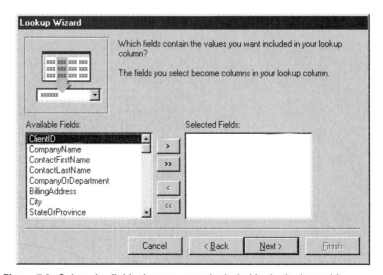

Figure 7.2 Select the fields that you want included in the lookup table

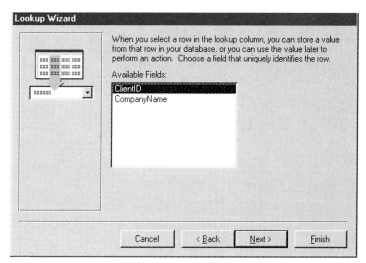

Figure 7.3 Pick the field that you want inserted into the record

You will not get a chance to choose a bound column if only one column is in the lookup table. If you hide the key column, the company name would appear in the orders table instead of the client ID number. We don't need to display the name because we're only using it as a link between the tables.

On your own, try to create a lookup field for the ShipBy field, so the valid shipper choices are displayed. Select the Wizard option that lets you enter the list values.

inserted into the order record? This is called the *bound column.* We want the ClientID, so make sure that field is selected and then click on Next. We're almost there.

The final Wizard dialog box asks for the label you want for the field. The default will be the field name, so let's leave it that way. You can also select to display help information about formatting fields. Just click on Finish. That's it.

Before seeing how the lookup field works, let's adjust one of its properties. First, notice that Access has set the Indexed property of the field to Yes (Duplicates OK). Now Click on the Lookup tab to see these options:

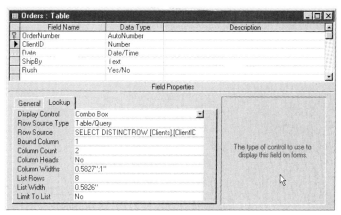

The Lookup Wizard has set these for you. They're not important unless you need to change them (a rather advanced operation). The properties create a combo box—that's a text box where you can enter information combined with a drop-down list. The Row Source Type and Row Source properties define where the information from the list is coming from. Bound Column specifies which column from the combo box contains the information to be inserted into the record. Column Count, Column Heads, and Column Widths specify how many columns there are, whether they have headings, and their width. List Rows is the number of values displayed in the list before scroll bars appears.

The List Width property is obvious. Auto sets the width to the same size as the column. Because we're showing two fields, and because the Company field may contain a long name, enter **1.5"** in the List Width property.

Now click in the Limit To List property. When this is set at No, you can type an entry into the text box that does not exist in the list. Since we're using the box to ensure that only valid client ID numbers are entered, we want to change this property. Click in the property box and enter Yes.

Click on the Table View button. Access displays a dialog box reporting that you must save the table; select Yes. A dialog box then appears asking if you want to check data integrity; select Yes. Now on your own add the following records to the table. As you do, however, try a rush order shipped by BOAT, and try to use a client number that does not exist. When you're done, close the table to return to the database window.

You can still type an entry for the field rather than select it from the list, but it must be a ClientID number actually in the Clients table.

Orders : Table

OrderNumber	ClientID	Order Date	ShipBy	Rush
1	1	2/2/96	AIR	☑
2	3	2/26/96	FEDEX	☑
3	1	3/14/96	DHL	☐
4	1	4/16/96	UPS	☑
5	6	4/29/96	UPS	☐
6	3	5/6/96	FEDEX	☑
7	4	5/1/96	DHL	☐
8	2	6/26/96	AIR	☐
9	5	7/6/96	UPS	☑
10	1	8/14/96	UPS	☐
11	4	8/19/96	AIR	☐
12	3	10/16/96	FEDEX	☑
13	3	11/11/96	UPS	☐
14	1	11/21/96	UPS	☐

Record: 1 of 14

SPEEDING SEARCHES WITH MULTIPLE FIELD INDEXES

Each of our tables has a primary key. As you know, you can create the primary key in Design View by selecting the field and then clicking on the Primary Key button. You can also create indexes for other fields by setting the Indexed property. Unlike the primary key, however, you have the option of using duplicate values in the indexed field. What we haven't mentioned so far is that the primary key or an index can be based on more than one field. We've been saving this little beauty for now.

Here's an example. Suppose you have a database of students in your computer training school. Because of some strange quirk of demographics, you have 50 students named Smith and 100 named Jones. You couldn't use the Last Name field as the primary key, because there are plenty of duplicates. (Chances are you'd be using an assigned student ID or the social security number as the primary key anyway.)

To speed searches using the student name, however, you could set the Last Name field to be indexed, with duplicates allowed. But because there are so many Smiths and Joneses, this wouldn't save Access a great deal of time, anyway. A more efficient method is to index combined fields to make duplicates less frequent, even if you cannot avoid them altogether. In this case, create an index using both the last and the first names.

Use multiple fields in an index to minimize the number of duplicates.

To see how this is done, create a multiple field index for the Clients table that you created earlier. The index combines the state and city of the contact's address to help you locate contacts based on their location. Open the Clients table in Design View. Now click on the Indexes button in the toolbar (or select Indexes from the View menu) to see the dialog box shown here.

Index Name	Field Name	Sort Order
▶ CompanyName	CompanyName	Ascending
ContactLastName	ContactLastName	Ascending
EmailAddress	EmailAddress	Ascending
PostalCode	PostalCode	Ascending
🔑 PrimaryKey	ClientID	Ascending

Index Properties

Primary	No	
Unique	No	The name for this index. Each index can use up to 10 fields.
Ignore Nulls	No	

Every index is assigned a name, a field that it is based on, and its sort order (either ascending or descending). The dialog box shows several indexes and a primary key that were already defined for you by Database Wizard.

To create a new index, you have to first give it a name. Click on the first blank row, under the Index Name column, and type **Location**. The name you choose really doesn't matter as long as it is not used by any other key or index. Just make it somehow identify the purpose of the index.

When you create a multiple field key, always start with the broadest field (the one that may provide the most duplicates) and work your way to the most narrow field. Click on the Field Name column in that row, pull down the list that appears to see the fields in the table, and select StateOrProvince.

Now before adding the next field to the index, look at the Index Properties. The three No values in this area mean that the index is not the primary key, it is not unique (duplicates are allowed), and that null values are not allowed. You do not want to make the index unique, because you may have more than one client in the same city.

OK, so much for the first part of the index. To add another field, move to the blank row under it and just select another field and sort order. Do not enter an index name, because this second field is part of the same index called Location. So in the next blank row under Field Name, pull down the list and select the City field.

Close the Indexes box, either by clicking on its Close box or on the Indexes button in the toolbar. When you're done, close the database, saving the changes.

BUILDING GOOD RELATIONSHIPS

We have skirted the issue of relationships several times. Relationships are important if your database is anything more than very simple.

We have two perfect candidates for a one-to-many relationship in the My Company database that we've been developing: the Clients and the Orders tables. Every client can have more than one order, which is why it's a one-to-many relationship. We should make the relationship official, sort of like marrying the tables, to prevent problems down the

Notice that the Index Properties do not appear when you're in a row that does not have an index name. The properties are associated with the index itself and not any individual field.

We'll discuss multiple field primary keys later.

We've taken care of that problem somewhat by making the ClientID field in the Orders table to be a lookup field from the Clients table. If you remember, we adjusted the property so if you did not select the client ID from the list you could only enter one that existed. Defining the relationship would do the same thing even without using a lookup table, but it goes much further.

When you create a table with Table Wizard, Access will suggest relationships if another table contains the same field name as the primary key.

If the Show Table dialog box does not appear, click on the Show Table button in the toolbar. You can use this button to add a table to the Relationships window at any time.

road. For example, we wouldn't want to create an order for a company not in our client's table—we haven't checked out their credit rating, and we don't have their address and other information on file.

A relationship solves some other types of problems too. Suppose the primary key for the Clients table is a type of field other than AutoNumber. This means you can change the value in a record's key field as long as it is unique. Without a relationship, you could assign a client a new ID number in the Clients table, but the ID number in their orders will not change. When you ask for a copy of their orders, none will print. With a relationship, changing the key value—the ID number—in the Clients table will automatically change it in all of the clients' orders.

The relationship also helps cure the repeating field blues, and it avoids problems when deleting records. For example, remember the hypothetical table earlier that included the names of members' children? The solution is two tables. One table has all of the members' general information. The other table contains their children's names. The two tables are related because they both refer to the member ID number.

Without a relationship, you could delete a member from one table but forget to delete the children from the other table. Database orphans. With a relationship, deleting the member automatically deletes the children as well.

OK, get the idea? To see how to get all of this magic together, let's define the relationship between the Clients and Orders tables.

Open the My Company database and then click on the Relationships button in the toolbar. If you already have the database open, you'll have to return to the database window to access the Relationships button. Access will display and open the Relationships window and display the Show Table dialog box showing the tables in the database, as shown here:

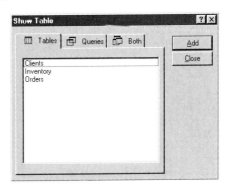

Double-click on Clients in the list. This places the table and a list of its fields in the Relationships window. Double-click on the Orders table also, then click on Close. The tables will appear in the Relationships window, as shown in Figure 7.4.

Now we want to relate the two tables using the ClientID fields. Point to the ClientID field in the Clients table list—the "one" side of the relationship—hold down the mouse, and drag to the ClientID field in the Orders table list. When you release the mouse button, Access displays the dialog box shown in Figure 7.5.

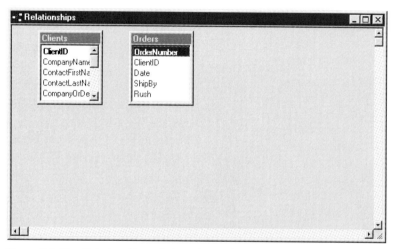

Figure 7.4 The Relationships window shows the tables that you are linking

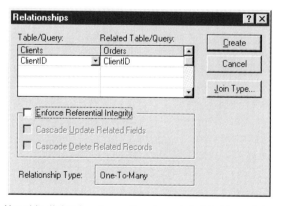

Figure 7.5 Use this dialog box to confirm the related fields and the type of relationship

The two fields can have different names as long as they are the same types and sizes. The field in the "one" table should be a primary key or a field that is indexed with no duplicates.

In database-speak, the "one" table is called the parent, and the "many" table is called the child.

The Table/Query list shows the name of the field in the "one" table. The Related Table/Query list shows the name of the field in the "many" table. If either is incorrect, click on the field name, pull down the list box, and select the correct field.

Next, decide if you want to Enforce Referential Integrity. Selecting this option is what really gives the relationship its power, making sure you cannot have a "many" record that does not match a "one" record, so click on that option now. This lets you select the other check boxes:

- Cascade Update Related Fields will update the ClientID in the orders to match changes to a client's ID in the client record.
- Cascade Delete Related Records will delete orders for clients deleted from the Clients table.

Both of these are certainly noble options, but we actually don't want either. The ClientID field is an AutoNumber type. We can't change it anyway, so we do not need the Cascade Update option. If we delete a client—because they no longer want to do business with us, for example—we do not want to delete their orders. Doing so may delete any record of outstanding orders that have not yet been paid for. Instant bankruptcy.

Finally, notice the setting in the Relationship Type box. It is set at One-To-Many. You can't change this option. Access defines the relationship based on the fields. If the field in the related ("many") table is defined as an index with no duplicates, then Access knows the relationship is one-to-one. Do you see why it has to be? Duplicates are not allowed, so there can only be one of each in the table. When the field in the related table can have duplicates, then Access knows the relationship is one-to-many.

Now click on Create. The Relationships window appears with the one-to-many relationship shown as a line from one field to the other:

The Join command determines how records from the two tables are combined when creating certain types of queries. You'll learn about this in Chapter 10.

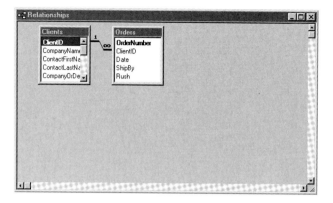

The 1 next to the Clients table indicates the "one" side of the relationship; the infinity symbol shows the "many" side. You cannot now enter a ClientID in the Orders table that does not exist in the Clients table. Close the Relationships window, saving the changes.

Working with Relationships

That's how relationships are formed when you don't have to place an ad in the personal section of the local paper. Now here are some ways to work with the Relationships window.

- To delete a relationship, click on the relationship line between tables and press DEL.
- To edit a relationship, double-click on the relationship line to display the Relationships dialog box.
- To hide a table from the Relationships window, click on it and press DEL. The table will no longer appear in the window, but its relationships are unaffected.
- To redisplay all relationships in the database, click on the Show All Relationships button.
- To see if a table has any hidden relationships, click on it and click on the Show Direct Relationships button.

ON YOUR OWN

Our database is lacking one very important table. The Orders table contains general information about each order but not the individual details, such as the item ordered and in what quantity. Since an order can be for more than one item, these would be repeating fields, a definite no-no. We need this information, however, to complete the order, so we need a table to store it.

On your own, create a table called Order Details with these fields:

Order Number	Number, indexed with duplicates allowed
ItemID	Number, indexed with duplicates allowed
Quantity	Number

Now create two lookup tables. For the OrderNumber field, select the OrderNumber and ClientID fields from the Orders table, using the OrderNumber field as the bound column—the column which contains the data that will be added to the table. This way, you can either enter or look up the order number. Follow the Lookup Wizard just as you did when you created the lookup column in the Orders table.

The other lookup table is for the ItemID field, and it will look up information in the Inventory table. When the Lookup Wizard asks you to select the fields, choose the Item field *first*, and then the ItemID field—you want the name of the item to appear first in the list. When the Wizard asks you to select the bound column (the field to enter into the table), select the ItemID field.

Access displays in the datasheet the contents of the first column in a lookup table. So, in this case, you'll see the full name of the item. However, it actually stores the contents of the bound column, which is the shorter item ID number. If you use the Find command to search through the column, for example, you search for ID numbers. When the Wizard is complete, edit the lookup properties like this:

General	Lookup
Display Control	Combo Box
Row Source Type	Table/Query
Row Source	SELECT DISTINCTROW [Inventory] [Item
Bound Column	2
Column Count	2
Column Heads	No
Column Widths	1.5";1"
List Rows	8
List Width	2.5"
Limit To List	Yes

Make certain the Column Widths, the List Width, and the Limit To List properties are set as shown.

Each record in the table will contain information about one item in one order. So if order number two is for five items, there will be five records, with the OrderNumber repeated in each. This creates a problem with the primary key. You cannot make the OrderID field the key, because it has duplicates. You also can't make the Item field the key, because several clients may order the same item. The trick is to find some combination of items that is unique. In this case, an item will only appear once in each order, so combine the OrderID and Item fields into the primary key.

When you combine fields into a primary key or into an index with no duplicates, only the combination must be unique. Each individual field can be duplicated, as long as it is not individually indexed without allowing duplicates.

Next, close the table and create relationships. Create a relationship between the OrderNumber field of the Orders table and the OrderNumber field of the Order Details table, enforcing referential integrity. Then create a relationship between the ItemID field in the Inventory table and the same field in the Order Details table, again enforcing referential integrity. The relationships should look like this:

To create a primary key on two fields, select them both (by dragging over consecutive row selectors, or using the CTRL key while you click) and then clicking on the Primary Key button.

Use the Show Table button to add the Order Details and Inventory tables to the Relationships window.

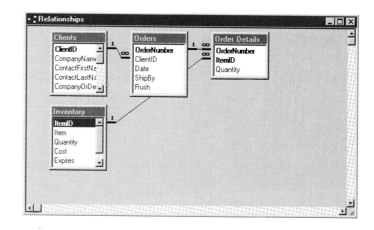

Finally, enter the records as shown in Figure 7.6.

DOCUMENTING YOUR WORK

Now that you've created your database and defined your tables, you might want a hard copy detailing your exhausting work. Keep it for your records in case your hard disk crashes or your backups are eaten

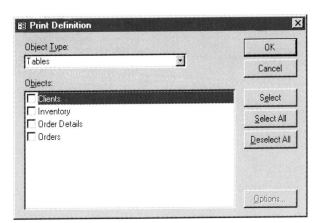

Figure 7.6 Enter these records into your table

by your pet iguana. The database Documentor can print a detailed report—sometimes in nauseating detail—showing the specifications of your database, tables, forms, reports, and other objects.

When you want to create a report, open the database and select Analyze from the Tools menu. Then click on Documentor to see the dialog box shown in Figure 7.7. To print a complete report, pull down the Object Type list and select All Object Types. You can also specify information just about the database in general, tables, forms, reports, macros, modules, and queries.

All of the objects—from the selected object types—will be shown in the Objects list. Click on Select All, or select the individual objects

You'll learn about the Table and Performance options in the Analyze menu in Chapter 11.

Figure 7.7 Use the Documentor to create a reference of your work

that you want to read about. To determine what gets printed about each object, select it and click on the Options button. Your choices depend on the object, but Figure 7.8 shows your choices for a table.

Finally, click on OK to create the report and to display it in a report window. Click on the Print button for a hardcopy reference.

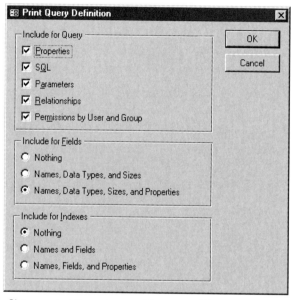

Figure 7.8 Choose what items to report for your tables

SO WHAT'S NEXT?

You know how to use them, now learn how to make them. Forms, that is. In Chapter 8, you'll learn how to create forms for your tables, even forms that use information from up to three related tables at the same time.

Creating Forms and Graphs with Form Wizard

FAST FORWARD

CREATE AN INSTANT FORM ➤ *pp 154-155*
1. Select the table in the database window.
2. Pull down the New Object button menu in the toolbar and click on AutoForm.

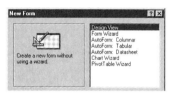

SELECT AN AUTOFORM STYLE ➤ *pp 156-157*
1. Click on the table in the database window.
2. Pull down the New Object button menu in the toolbar and click on New Form.
3. Select AutoForm: Columnar, AutoForm: Tabular, or AutoForm: Datasheet, and then click on OK.
4. Save and close the Form.

USE FORM WIZARD ➤ *pp 157-159*
1. Click on the Forms tab in the database window and select New.
2. Click on Form Wizard, and then on OK.
3. Select the table and fields, then click on Next.
4. Select Columnar, Tabular, or Datasheet, and then click on Next.
5. Choose the style, and then click on Next.
6. Enter a form title, and select if you want to open the form or show it in Design View.
7. Click on Finish to see the form.

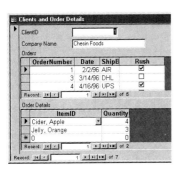

CREATE A FORM WITH SUBFORMS ➤ *pp 162-163*

1. Click on the Forms tab and select New.
2. Click on Form Wizard, and then on OK.
3. Select the parent table and fields, and then select the child table and fields.
4. Select a second child table and fields, and then click on Next.
5. Select how you want to look at the form, and if you want subforms or linked forms, and then click on Next.
6. Select the look for each subform, and then click on Next.
7. Select a style for the form, and then click on Next.
8. Enter the form and subform titles, and click on Finish.

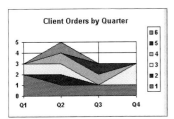

CREATE A CHART ➤ *pp 163-166*

1. Click on the Forms tab and select New.
2. Choose the table, click on Chart Wizard, and then on OK.
3. Select the fields to chart, and then click on Next.
4. Select the chart type, and then click on Next.
5. Choose the x-axis and y-axis fields, and then click on OK.
6. Enter a chart title, and choose if you want to include a legend, then click on Finish.

Forms are a great way to enter and edit information in your database. They're orderly and consistent, they're not intimidating, and they're easy to work with. So when you create your own table, probably one of the first things you'll want to do is to create a form. Remember all of the ways that Access gave you to make tables? You have even more ways to create forms. There's even one way that takes just two clicks. In fact, we recommend getting into the habit of making one of these two-click forms for every table you create. Then you have the immediate choice of using a datasheet or a form to work with information. In this chapter, we'll show you how to create forms in several ways, and how to create eye-catching charts and graphs.

CREATING INSTANT FORMS

The quickest way to create a form is with AutoForm. You just tell Access what table you want to use, and Access does all of the rest. Here's all you have to do.

That's it. Try it now using the Clients table of the My Company database. Click on Clients in the database window, pull down the New Object button menu, and select AutoForm. Access creates what's called a columnar form and opens it so you can start using it. A columnar form for the Clients table looks as shown in Figure 8.1. The form contains all of the table's fields, and you see one record at a time onscreen. Click on the Save button in the toolbar, type the form name—let's call it Clients—and then click on OK. Now close the form to return to the database window.

CAUTION

You must have a table selected in the database window to create an AutoForm.

INSTANT FORMS step by step

1. Click on the table in the database window.

2. Pull down the New Object button menu and select AutoForm.

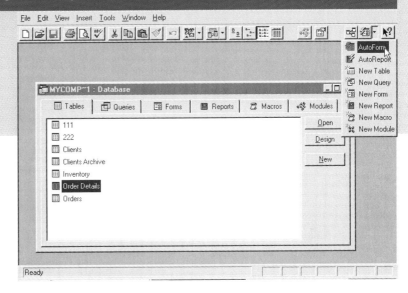

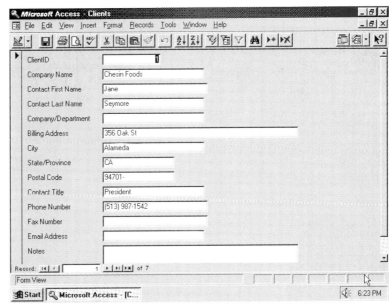

Figure 8.1 A columnar form lists all of the fields down the screen

CHOOSING AN AUTOFORM STYLE

Just as in the fast food business, instant doesn't have to mean lack of choice. You don't have to settle for one type of form just because you're too busy to design the form yourself from scratch. Have it your way. When you use the New Form command, you can select one of three styles of AutoForms as well as other ways to create even more sophisticated forms. Select New Form from either the New Object button menu in the toolbar, or by clicking on New in the Forms page of the database window. Access will display this dialog box:

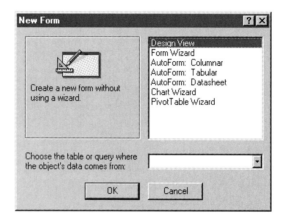

To see the AutoForm options, select the table to use for the basis for the form. If you selected New Form when a table was open in the foreground window, or you selected in the database window, then the table's name will automatically appear in the dialog box. If no name appears, or the name of the wrong table appears, then pull down the list and select the table that you want to use.

Next, decide which of the three AutoForm styles you want. In addition to columnar, you can select tabular and datasheet. In a tabular form, the fields appear across the screen like columns, so you can see more than one record at a time—although you may have to scroll left and right to see all of the fields. A datasheet form looks just like a datasheet.

Go figure. The AutoForm: Datasheet option displays a datasheet, just as if you had opened the table. However, it actually creates a tabular form containing just one record at a time. If you pull down the Form

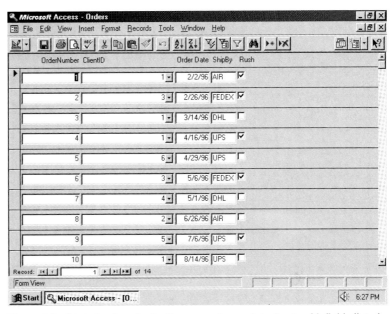

Figure 8.2 A tabular form looks like a very fancy datasheet, with fields listed across the top of the screen

View button and select Form View, you'll see the form as a form. Use this option if you want a tabular layout for single records.

Let's now create a tabular form for the Orders table. The Tables page is already displayed, so click on the Orders table, pull down the New Object button menu in the toolbar, and click on New Form to display the dialog box. The name of the selected table should appear in the text box. If not, pull down the list and select the Orders table.

Click on AutoForm: Tabular, and then on OK. Review the form when it appears (Figure 8.2). Click on Save, type a form name—let's call it List of Orders—and then click on OK. Now close the form to return to the database window.

USING FORM WIZARD

Columnar, tabular, and datasheet are the Moe, Larry, and Curly of the form world. They're great fun to have around, but would you trust your business to them? When you want an award-winning performance, try Form Wizard. Like other wizards, Form Wizard lets you select options so you can customize the form's appearance. It only takes a few steps, so it's not really any more difficult or time-consuming than AutoForm.

SHORTCUT

You do not have to first select a table, since you'll have the opportunity in the Wizard dialog box. However, if you do pick a table now, its fields will be shown in the first Form Wizard dialog box automatically.

CAUTION

Do not add fields from more than one table if the tables are not related with referential integrity.

We'll make two forms using Form Wizard. The first is a simple columnar form for the Clients table. Instead of using all of the fields, however, we'll just use selected ones. This time, we'll use the New option from the Forms page of the database window, just for a little variety.

1. Click on the Forms tab.
2. Click on New.
3. Click on Form Wizard.
4. Click on OK.

The first Wizard dialog box (Figure 8.3) asks you to choose the fields that you want in the form. The box includes a message that says you can select fields from more then one source; we'll use fields from several tables later on. You add fields just as you learned when using Table Wizard.

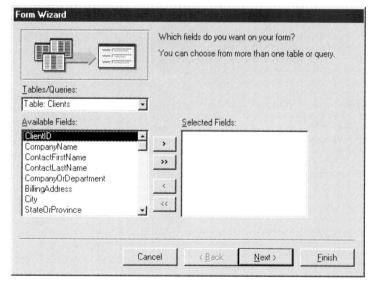

Figure 8.3 In the first Form Wizard dialog box, choose the fields that you want displayed

1. If Table: Clients is not listed in the Tables/Queries box, pull down the list and select it now.
2. Click on the ClientID field and then on the > button.
3. In the same way, add the fields CompanyName, ContactFirstName, ContactLastName, and PhoneNumber.

4. Click on Next. In the next dialog box, you can select the type of form: Columnar, Tabular, or Datasheet.

5. Click on Tabular and then on Next. You must now select the style of the form. The option will already be set at your last choice either from Form Wizard or from Database Wizard. If you last selected the International style in Database Wizard, for example, that same style will be selected here.

6. Click on Standard and then on Next. In this final dialog box, enter a form title, and select if you want to open the form or show it in Design View, or show help information.

7. Type **Clients Tabular** and then click on Finish to see the form. It is a tabular form, much like the one created by AutoForm: Tabular, but only with the selected fields.

Close the form when you're done admiring your handiwork.

If you create a form with fewer than all of the fields, as you just did, the form still works as explained in Chapter 2. You can still use the form to display information from the table, as well as to edit it and add new records. Of course, you'll only be able to see, edit, or add the fields displayed in the form. When you add a new record, for example, fields not on the form will be blank. Because of this, you must add the primary key field to the form if you plan to use it to add records when the primary key is not an AutoNumber type.

When you're done examining your new form, close it. You do not have to save it first—Form Wizard has already done that for you.

Creating Forms from Multiple Tables

Now for something really special. Let's create a form that takes advantage of the relationships between tables. Picture this. You want to review orders placed by clients. If you just open the Orders table, you'll see the overall order information but not the client's name (ID only) and none of the individual item details. That's not very nice. You'd also like to write the details of an order while viewing some information from the Clients and Orders table all on the same screen. This requires what's called a form/subform. The form refers to the "one" table, and the subform to the "many" table. In this form, we'll have two subforms—one for the Orders table and another for the Order Details table.

CAUTION

In order to create a form/subform, the tables must have a one-to-many relationship, with referential integrity enforced. If not, it's a no-no, and Access will display a message telling you so.

Note the nuances here. When comparing the Clients and Orders table, Clients is on the one side of the relationship and Orders is on the many side. If you consider the Orders and Order Details tables, however, Orders is now on the one side and Order Details is on the many side.

upgrade note

You no longer need to create a multiple table query or use Design View to create a form with subforms. Access can do it for you using Form Wizard.

Creating a form/subform is easy. In fact, it works the same as a simple form. The difference is that you select fields from multiple tables, and then select the style of the subforms. There are a number of steps involved, so let's do it step by step.

1. Click on the Forms tab.
2. Click on New.
3. Click on Form Wizard.
4. Pull down the table list and select Clients.
5. Click on OK to see the Wizard dialog box where you select fields.
6. Click on ClientID, and then on >.
7. Click on CompanyName, and then on >.
8. Pull down the table list and select Table: Orders. The fields in the Orders table are now listed.
9. Add the OrderNumber, Date, ShipBy, and Rush fields to the list.
10. Pull down the table list and select Table: Order Details.
11. Add the ItemID and Quantity fields to the list.
12. Click on Next. In this next dialog box (Figure 8.4), you select how you want to view the form.

By default, the form will be divided into three distinct areas, as shown in the preview panel on the right. There'll be a separate area for the fields from each of the three tables—three separate (but related) forms on the same page. You can also decide to have fewer sections or distinct form areas. If you want to combine the first two tables into one section, for example, click on by Orders. There would then be just two sections: the fields from both Clients and Orders are in one section;

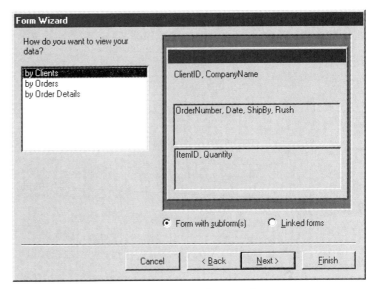

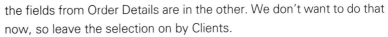

Figure 8.4 Choose how you want to organize your data

the fields from Order Details are in the other. We don't want to do that now, so leave the selection on by Clients.

You can also select to have subforms or linked forms. With subforms, all of the forms appear onscreen. If you select linked forms, then a button appears rather than the subforms—just click on the button when you want the subform information to appear.

1. Click on Next. You now must choose a look for each subform, either tabular or datasheet (Figure 8.5). Clicking on an option will show how it appears in the preview area. The main form, by the way, is always columnar. Leave the options set at the default, which is Datasheet.

2. Click on Next. The box appears to select a style.

3. Choose a style that suits your mood and then click on Next. You can now name the form and each of the subforms. When you open the main form, all of the subforms appear as well. The subforms will also, however, appear listed separately in the database window. You can also choose to open the form in Form View or Design View, and to show help information.

4. Type **Clients and Order Details** as the form name, and then click on Finish to see the completed form (Figure 8.6).

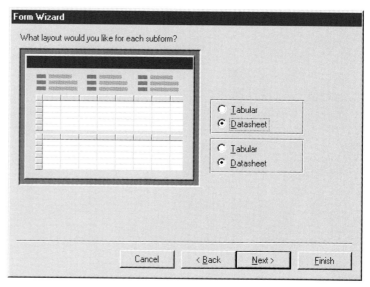

Figure 8.5 Select the appearance of each subform

You could have also added the Cost field from the Inventory database to see the cost of each item. However, unless you change the form in Design View, a user could change the cost. In most cases, the cost is not changed when taking orders, so we left that field out for now.

Working with Subforms

There's an awful lot on your screen, but don't be intimidated. Take your time. There are actually three forms displayed, each representing one of three tables. Also notice that there are three sets (count 'em!)

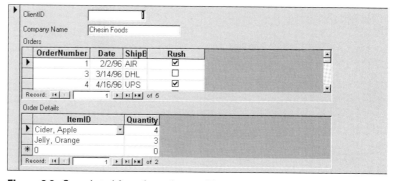

Figure 8.6 Completed form from three tables

of navigation buttons. Each set controls one form, and thus the records in one table.

The buttons at the very bottom of the form control the main form—the records from the Clients table. As you select another client, the client information appears in the top of the form, and the orders appear in the Orders section. The details of the selected order appear in the Order Details section.

To see the details of another order, select it in the Order section. To see the order for another client, change to that client record.

To add a new record, you have to decide which table you want to add it to:

You can apply a sort order and filter to each section of the form.

- To add another client, for example, click on the Add Record button at the bottom of the form. You can also click in any of the fields from the Client table and then use the New Record button in the toolbar.
- To add an order, first display the client, and then click on the New Record button in the Order subform (or, click on an Order field and use the New Record button in the toolbar).
- To add details, make sure the focus is on the correct order as shown in the Orders section, and then click on the New Record button in the Order Details section.

Use the same procedure to display or change information. Work your way from selecting the proper client, then the order, and then the order details.

Now on your own, play around with the form. Change records, add information, and experiment until you feel comfortable with how the form works. When you're done, close the form. The wizard has saved the form for you, and Access automatically saves each record that you create or modify.

EMPHASIZING INFORMATION IN CHARTS

Charts can be addictive, and like many things in life get overused. How many slick magazines and newspapers do you see with charts that are so fancy and junked-up that you can't make any sense out of them? A chart is supposed to make it easier to interpret information, and it can't when it's designed like a tie-dyed inkblot test.

In order to use Chart Wizard you must include the Developer Tools using the Custom option when you install Access. See Appendix A for more information.

With that pet peeve out of the way, we can now look at Chart Wizard. Chart Wizard is similar to Form Wizard. You get to select which fields you want to include and how you want the form to appear. The difference is that Chart Wizard presents your data in a graph.

Before jumping into a chart, you should understand some charting terminology. Look at Figure 8.7. This simple chart shows the number of dollars spent in each quarter of the year. The quarters are shown along the x-axis, which is represented by the horizontal line. The x-axis is sometimes called the category axis. Each bar in the chart represents the amount of money spent in one quarter. The amounts spent are shown in a scale along the y-axis, which is represented by the vertical line. The y-axis is sometimes called the value axis. When you create a chart, you tell Access which fields you want to chart, and which to use as the x-axis and the y-axis. The y-axis field, by the way, must contain numbers or currency amounts.

Chart Wizard produces a chart that you can customize in Design View. The capabilities are much like those available in Word and Excel.

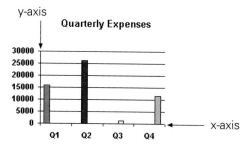

Figure 8.7 Knowing the parts of a chart makes them easier to create

Now a friendly warning. It may take some trial and error to produce the chart that you have in mind. If your chart doesn't look right, just try making another, and then another, and so on until you get it right.

As an example, we will make a basic chart showing the number of orders placed by each client by the quarters of the year. Click on the Forms tab, select New, and then click on Chart Wizard. Pull down the table list at the bottom of the dialog box, choose Orders, and then click on OK to see the Wizard dialog box where you select fields. Add the ClientID and the Date fields and then click on Next. You now select the type of chart, as shown in Figure 8.8.

For this example, click on Next to accept the default Column chart type. In the next dialog box (Figure 8.9), you designate how you want to chart the information.

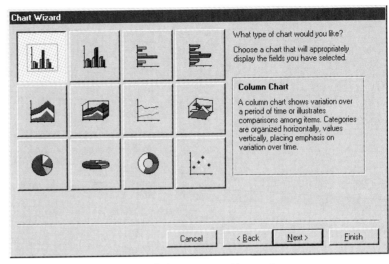

Figure 8.8 Choose the type of chart you want to create

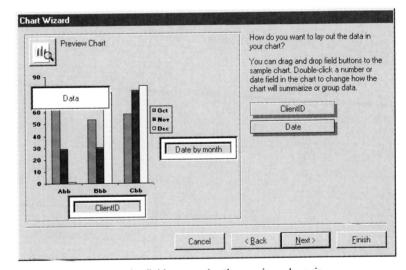

Figure 8.9 Designate the fields to use for the x-axis and y-axis

As you move and adjust fields, the sample chart will change to reflect the new settings. However, don't trust what you see on the screen; it's just a rough sample of the type of chart that will be created.

The fields that you've selected will be listed on the right. Access tries to guess how you want to create the chart and selects an x-axis and y-axis field for you. In this case, Access got a little confused. First, we want to count the number of times each client ordered in a month. So drag ClientID from the right side of the box to the Data box. It should read CountOfClientID.

Just as you double-clicked on Date by month to select another way to use it in the chart, you can also double-click on the data item to select ways to organize data.

Next, we want to change how Access uses the other fields. We want to use the date for the x-axis, so drag Date from the right side of the box to where it says ClientID under the x-axis. It will appear as Date by month. To display the date by quarters, double-click on the Date by month notation to see this dialog box:

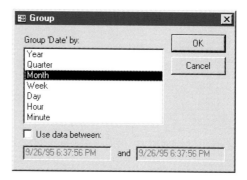

Select Quarter in the list box that appears and then OK. Finally, drag ClientID from the right side of the box to where it says Date by month—where the legend will appear.

Click on Preview Chart for a quick look at the chart so far. Click on Close in the preview to return to Chart Wizard.

Now click on Next. In the next Wizard dialog box, you enter a title for the chart and select whether you want to include a legend. You can also choose to display the chart or modify it. Type **Chart of Orders** as the form name, and then select Finish to see the completed chart (Figure 8.10).

As your chart is being made, Chart Wizard will display a default datasheet and chart showing figures for four quarters. Don't pay any attention to it now. You'll learn more about this default chart later.

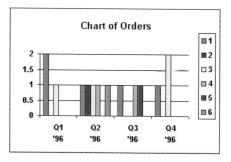

Figure 8.10 Your completed chart has more impact than a printed table

Click on Save, type **Orders by Quarter**, and then click on OK.

Modifying a Chart

If you've worked with charts in Excel or Word, then you'll feel right at home—the techniques are about the same.

Click on the Design View button to show the chart in Design View (we won't actually be dealing with that now—we're saving Design View for later). Now double-click on the chart. Windows opens the Microsoft Graph application, as shown in Figure 8.11. This is the program that actually created the chart for you.

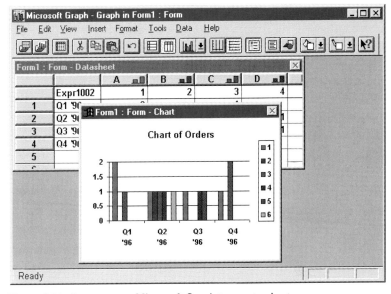

Figure 8.11 Access uses Microsoft Graph to create charts

You'll see the chart window with your chart. Behind the chart is a datasheet (although it doesn't look like an Access datasheet) containing the charted information. The window also contains the Graph menu bar and toolbar. The File, Window, and Help menu items contain the same options as those in a document window. Table 8-1 shows the new functions available in the menus. Table 8-2 shows the functions of the toolbar.

Click on the View Datasheet button to display it in the foreground. The datasheet is just like a spreadsheet, but the row headings appear in the column to the left of column A, and column headings appear in the row above row 1.

Menu	Functions
File	Return to Access
Edit	Import data or a chart from a spreadsheet program and perform editing techniques such as cut, copy, and paste
View	Switch between the datasheet and graph, select toolbars, and zoom the display
Insert	Add cells, titles, data labels, a legend, axis labels, grid lines, and trend lines
Format	Format the appearance of text and chart elements, the column width, chart type, and 3-D View
Tools	Display options for selecting default colors and graph type, to allow drag and drop of cells, and to move the insertion point to a new cell when you press ENTER
Data	Display data series from row or column information, and include or exclude specific rows or columns
Help	Get information on the Graph application

Table 8.1 Microsoft Graph Menu Options

Toolbar Button	Button Name	Function
	Import Data	Import data from another document, table, or spreadsheet
	Import Chart	Import a chart from a spreadsheet program
	View Datasheet	Toggle between the datasheet and the graph
	Cut	Cut
	Copy	Copy
	Paste	Paste
	Undo	Undo
	By Row	Choose data series from rows
	By Column	Choose data series from columns
	Chart Type	Select the chart type

Table 8.2 Microsoft Graph Toolbar Buttons

Toolbar Button	Button Name	Function
	Vertical Gridlines	Turn on or off vertical grid lines
	Horizontal Gridlines	Turn on or off horizontal grid lines
	Legend	Turn on or off the legend
	Text Box	Create a text box
	Drawing	Display the drawing toolbar for drawing on the graph
	Color	Choose a color for graph objects
	Pattern	Choose a pattern for graph objects
	Help	Get context-sensitive help

Table 8.2 Microsoft Graph Toolbar Buttons (*continued*)

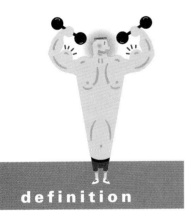

definition

Handles: *Small boxes around a selected object used to change the object size.*

While Access maintains a link between the table and the chart, Microsoft Graph does not. If you change the row or column headings or the values in the Graph application, you'll see the new information in the chart window and while in Design View. But when you switch to Form View, the data from the table will appear charted.

Bring the chart back to the foreground by clicking on the View Datasheet button again. While you cannot change the information in the chart, you can use the toolbar and the menu bar options to change its appearance.

For example, click on the title of the chart. The title will appear surrounded by a frame with handles. Drag over the text in the title and type **Client Orders by Quarter**. Now, pull down the Chart Type button and select the area type chart—the top button on the left side.

If you had wanted to use the quarters for the legend and the ClientID for the x-axis, click on the By Column button.

Finally, click on the Vertical Gridlines button to display vertical lines at the quarter indicators on the x-axis. Choose Exit and Return from the File menu to return to Design View, and then click on Form View to see how the form now appears. The chart now shows the accumulated number of orders for all clients in an order. Individual clients are represented by the area sections. Click on Save to save the chart, and then close it to return to the database window.

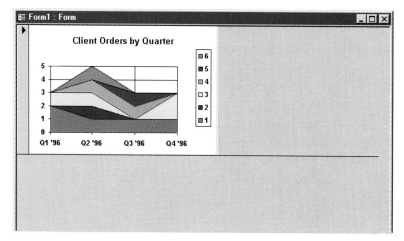

Now on Your Own

When you have some time, return to Design View and experiment with the menu bar and toolbar to learn more about creating graphs. Select the form in the Form pages of the database window, click on Design, and then double-click on the chart.

You can select or change the type of graph by selecting an option from the Chart Type list. Two-dimensional graphs are on the left side of the list, and three-dimensional types are on the right. For each type of graph you can also choose from predefined formats. Choose Auto-Format from the Format menu, for example, to display this dialog box:

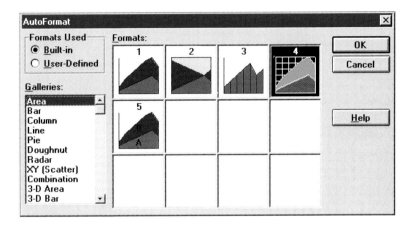

As you pick a chart type in the Galleries list of this dialog box, subtypes of it will appear in the box's Format list. Choose the chart type and subtype, and then click on OK.

You can also choose a subtype and customize a chart by selecting Chart Type from the Format menu, and then clicking on Options in that dialog box that appears.

To customize the rotation, elevation, and other aspects of a three-dimensional graph, choose 3-D View from the Format menu to see its dialog box.

You can format any part of the chart by selecting it and then choosing an option from the Format menu. You can also double-click on a part of the chart for its format options.

Also experiment with the Chart Wizard. Try different arrangements of fields in the data, series, and axis positions.

SO WHAT'S NEXT?

While you can print out forms, they are really designed to view and change information on the screen. Reports, on the other hand, are meant to be printed and distributed. Reports can even help you analyze your information, as you will learn in Chapter 9.

Creating Reports

FAST FORWARD

CREATE AN INSTANT REPORT ➤ *pp 176-177*

1. Select the table in the database window.
2. Pull down the New Object button in the toolbar and click on AutoReport.

SELECT AUTOREPORT STYLES ➤ *pp 177-178*

1. Click on the table in the database window.
2. Pull down the New Object button menu in the toolbar and click on New Report.
3. Choose AutoReport: Columnar or AutoReport: Tabular, and then click on OK.
4. Save and close the report.

USE REPORT WIZARD ➤ *pp 179-181*

1. Click on the Report tab, and then on New.
2. Click on Report Wizard, and then on OK.
3. Select the table and fields, then click on Next.
4. If using fields from related tables, select overall grouping for sections, then click on Next.
5. Select the field or fields to group by and grouping options, then click on Next.
6. In the series of dialog boxes that appear, choose sort fields, layout options, and the overall style, clicking on Next when you complete each box.
7. Enter a report title, and select if you want to show the report in Print Preview or Design View, and then click on Finish to see the report.

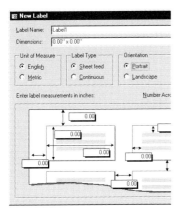

LABEL WIZARD ➤ *pp 181-185*

1. Display the Reports page of the database window and click on New.
2. Select Label Wizard.
3. Select the table to use for the labels, and then click on OK.
4. Choose a predefined format of your label size or create a custom label size, then click on Next.
5. Select the font, font size, weight, and style to use for label text, and then click on Next.
6. Arrange the layout of fields on the label prototype, and then click on Next.
7. Select one or more fields for sorting, then click on Next.
8. Type a report title, and then click on Finish to see the labels in Print Preview.

Maybe you don't want to admit it, but we're all just a little too neurotic to really trust a paperless world. We like to see a real signature on a contract and feel that grain between our fingers. Sure, we can do without the paper cuts and stapling fingers while trying to separate pages for copying. Perhaps it's just instinctive, an unconscious reminder of the primordial forests of distant ancestors, but some of us just trust paper more.

Microsoft must feel the same way or at least be in synch with these feelings, because they've given us reports. Reports are meant to be printed, passed around, and bound in books. And they're so quick. You create reports just as you do forms. The only difference is that you use the AutoReport or New Report options from the New Object list or select New from the Reports page of the database window. If you've done forms, you can do reports.

Like a form and a datasheet, the information you see when you preview (open) a report depends on what's actually in the table. Once you create a report, it will always show you the current contents of the underlying table. You only have to create a new report when you want a different layout or design.

CREATING AN INSTANT REPORT

Try it now. Start Access and open the My Company database. Click on the Inventory table, pull down the New Object list and click on AutoReport. Simple.

AutoReport creates the columnar report (Figure 9.1). This means that all of the record's fields are listed in a column down the page. The report is rather sparse, with no heading, date, or page number, but it does show the contents of the table. Access will place one record after the next, but it will not divide a record between pages. If a record has

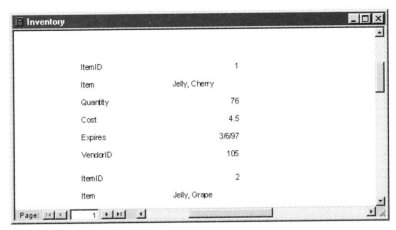

Figure 9.1 Create an instant columnar report with AutoReport

more fields than can fit on one page, however, it will divide them between pages and start each record on a new page.

Select Save from the File menu, type a name for your report—we'll use **Basic Inventory**—and then click on OK. Click on Close to switch to Design View. Pull down the View button menu to see the options Design View, Print Preview, and Layout Preview. Design View, as you know, lets you change the layout and design of the report. Print Preview shows you how the report will appear when printed. Layout Preview is only available for reports. Layout Preview collects just enough of the actual information to see a sample of how the report will appear. It is faster than Print Preview when you have a large table, but use it only for a quick look at the report's structure and not to see what actually will be printed.

Select Close from the File menu.

Creating Fancier Instant Reports

While the report you just created was rather plain looking, you can create better looking instant reports as well. Just use the New command from the Reports page of the Database window (or choose New Report from the New Object button in the toolbar) to see this dialog box:

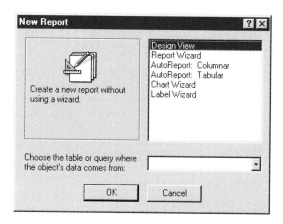

Chart Wizard works exactly the same for reports as it does for forms. Enough said.

Landscape: *Printing across the long edge of the page.*

You have two AutoReport options—columnar and tabular. Using AutoReport from the New Report menu takes a few more steps than using the New Object button, and the reports take longer to generate, but it has a definite advantage. The reports are more formatted, as shown in Figure 9.2. The table name appears as the report heading, and the date and page number, along with the total number of pages, appears at the bottom of each page. In a tabular report, the fields are listed across the top of the page, like column headings. The report will print in landscape orientation, and Access will try to print as many fields on a page as possible, even clipping some of the field names. Extra columns will print on another page.

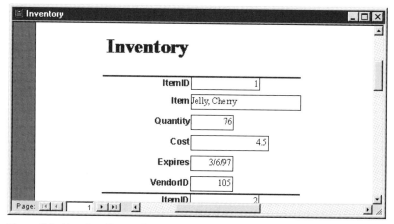

Figure 9.2 Use AutoReport from the New Report dialog box for better looking instant output

REPORT WIZARD

If you want more control over the design of your report without getting bogged down in report design, then use Report Wizard. Like Form Wizard, it lets you select fields and style options, and you can even create reports with fields from related tables. Start Report Wizard now by selecting it from the New Report box, and then click on OK.

In the first Wizard dialog box, you select the fields that you want to add to the report, including fields from related tables. From the Clients table, add the ClientID, CompanyName, BillingAddress, City, StateOrProvince, and PostalCode fields. From the Orders table, add the OrderNumber and Date fields. From the Order Details table, add the Quantity field. And from the Inventory table, add the Item and Cost fields, and then click on Next.

Since you have selected fields from multiple tables, the next Report Wizard dialog box (Figure 9.3) then lets you choose their grouped arrangement, which is the same as grouping fields for forms and subforms. If you recall, this lets you select if you want the fields from each table listed separately or grouped together.

The suggested grouping is ideal: the client information will appear first, then the order information, and finally the details for the order, including the name and the cost of the item. Click on Next.

Click on the Show me more information button to learn more about relationships and grouping reports.

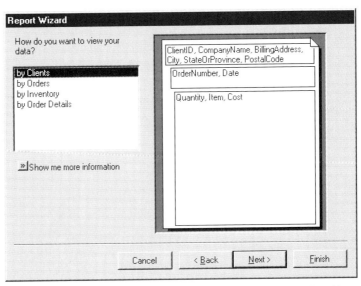

Figure 9.3 Choose the group arrangement for reports from multiple tables

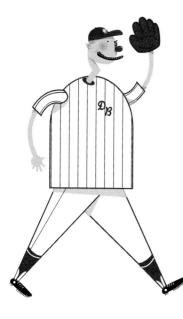

The next dialog box lets you choose if you want to organize the information by any other groups. Click on Next. When you do not group by a field, the records appear one after the other. Grouping by a field lets you divide the report into sections—not by tables but by the values in the selected field.

You can group on more than one field. For example, if you are interested in when clients placed orders, you could first group by ClientID—so all of a client's orders are listed together—and then by date—so they are in date order for each client. You could also group first by date and then by contact for each date. It all depends on how you want to view the records. In addition to selecting the fields for grouping, you can also select grouping options. By default, dates are grouped by month, but for all other fields each unique field value is another group—each ClientID, each Last Name, and so on. This is called normal grouping. Grouping Options lets you change what is considered a group.

With a date field, for example, you can also select to group by year, quarter, day, or some other interval. You can also select "normal" to use each unique date. For numeric and currency fields you can select normal, or by 10s, 50s, and so on. Text fields can be grouped normally, by the first letter of each value (for an index-type listing, such as As, Bs, and so on) or by some number of initial characters.

For a sample of grouping by the first character, add data to the Contact Management database and then preview the Alphabetical Contact Listing report. Preview the Weekly Call Summary report to see dates grouped by their week. (This report has a special feature that lets you designate the range of dates you want to include—enter the dates 1/1/95 and 12/31/95.)

The next Report Wizard dialog box lets you sort on up to four fields. This same box lets you choose summary options, so you can calculate and display the sum, average, minimum, or maximum values for each group. For example, suppose you group the orders by ClientID. If you select the Count summary option, the report will show the number of orders for each client. You can also decide to show the details and summary (such as information about each specific order, as well as the count of orders), or just summary information only (just the count for each client). Choose a sort order, if you want it, and then click on Next.

Some of the objects—such as CompanyName and BillingAddress— are too small to display the complete field name. You'll have to adjust the report in Design View, as you'll learn how to do in Chapter 13.

Another Report Wizard dialog box lets you choose the layout for the details in the report, including portrait or landscape orientation, and lets you adjust field width so all fields fit on a page. Select a style that suits your mood and then click on Next. In the Wizard dialog box, you select the overall style of the report—take your pick and then click on Next. You can now enter a report title, and choose if you want it to appear in Print Preview or Design View. Type **Client Orders** as the report title, and then click on Finish to see the report in Print Preview (Figure 9.4). Note that the label Order Date is used for the Date field because it was specified as a caption property when the field was defined for the table. If you scroll the report, you'll also see that StateOrProvince has the label State/Province.

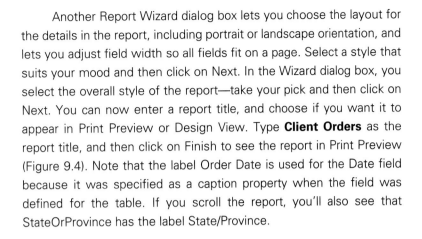

Figure 9.4 Completed report in Print Preview

Report Wizard saves your report for you. AutoReport doesn't.

The report includes all of the information, although it could not be used to print invoices. The extended price has not been calculated, nor the totals for each order. We'll take care of that later. Choose Close in the File menu to return to the database window.

LABEL WIZARD

Use the Label Wizard for name badges, shelf labels, and other labeling tasks, in addition to mailing labels.

If you need to print mailing labels from your table, then you'll love Label Wizard. Like all wizards, you select options from a series of dialog boxes. In this case, you select the label format and the arrangement of fields on the label.

The best way to learn it is to use it. So let's create mailing labels for the people in the Clients table. Display the Reports page of the database window and click on New. Select Label Wizard, pull down the table list, choose Clients, and then click on OK.

In the first Wizard dialog box (Figure 9.5), you must select the labels that you are using. We're going to use the Avery 5096 label, so click on that option now. But if you want a different form, select the label type (either sheet feed or continuous), choose the units of measure, and then scroll the list to select the specific form. For now, click on Next.

If none of the predefined labels are correct, click on Customize. You'll see a dialog box where you can define your own custom label sizes. To create a new size, click on the New button in that dialog box. Another box appears where you enter the specifications for your label, including its type, size, number across the page, and details about its spacing on the page and in relation to other labels.

The next Wizard dialog box lets you choose the font, font size, weight, style, and color for the label text. The default is Arial, 8-point, light. Click on the Font Name list in the dialog box, scroll the list of fonts, and select Times New Roman. Make your choices from the options and then click on Next.

CAUTION

If you select too large a font size, your information may not fit on the labels.

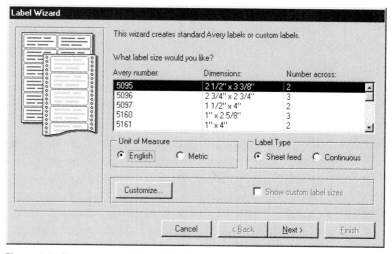

Figure 9.5 Choose a predefined label format, or create your own

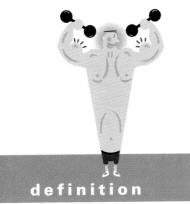

Now you must arrange the fields on the label using the dialog box shown in Figure 9.6. Since we're creating a mailing label, we want a standard address format. You add a field to the label in much the same way you add fields to forms and reports. Double-click on ContactFirstName in the Available Fields list, or click on it once and then on the > button. Access moves the field to the Prototype label and surrounds it in braces.

There is no < button to remove a field from the prototype. To remove a field, drag over it with the mouse and then press the DEL key.

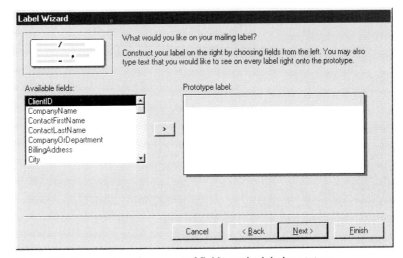

Figure 9.6 Arrange the placement of fields on the label prototype

After you move a field to the prototype, the next field in the list is automatically selected. Before adding the ContactLastName field, however, press SPACEBAR. This will insert a space between the names in the label. Double-click on ContactLastName to add it to the label, and then press ENTER to move to the next line in the prototype.

Now add the BillingAddress field to the prototype and press ENTER, then add the City field. Type a comma and a space after the City field, add the StateOrProvince field, type two spaces, and then add the PostalCode field. The completed prototype will look like this:

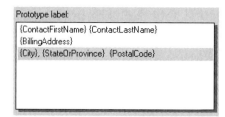

Prototype label:

{ContactFirstName} {ContactLastName}
{BillingAddress}
{City}, {StateOrProvince} {PostalCode}

Click on Next. The next dialog box lets you select one or more fields to sort the labels by. You can use any of the fields in the table, even those not on the label itself. Since we want to take advantage of bulk rates, double-click on the PostalCode field to add it to the Sort By list, and then click on Next.

The final Wizard dialog box asks if you want to see the labels in Print Preview or Design View. Leave the option set to the default: See the labels as they will look printed. Type **Labels** for the report name, and then click on Finish to see the labels as shown in Figure 9.7.

If you look closely at the preview you'll notice that nine-digit zip codes do not have a hyphen following the first five numbers.

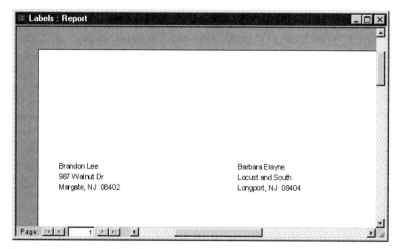

Figure 9.7 Labels in Print Preview

Choose Close from the File menu to return to the database window. When you're ready to print labels, just select the report, get your labels ready in the printer, and click on the Print button.

SO WHAT'S NEXT?

Recording information into a database program and displaying it in forms and reports is nice, but what good is it? You could do the same with a good typist and file clerk. The real important work of a database program is to help you find specific information when you need it, and to help make important decisions. You'll start learning how to perform these wonders with queries in Chapter 10.

CHAPTER 10

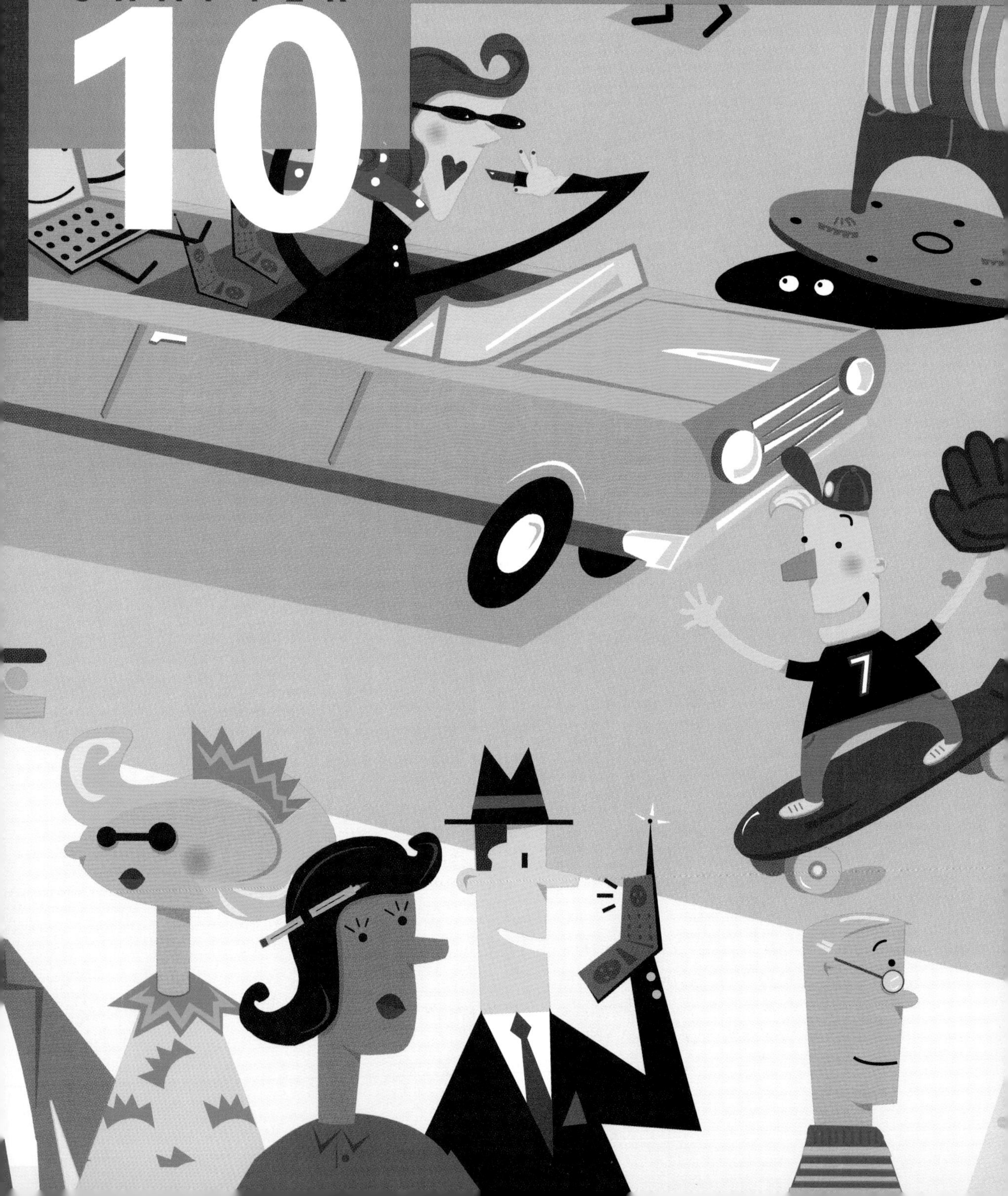

Finding Information with Queries

FAST FORWARD

Simple Query Wizard

Which fields do y
You can choose

Tables/Queries:
Table: Clients

Available Fields: Selected I
ClientID
CompanyName
ContactFirstName
ContactLastName
CompanyOrDepartment
BillingAddress
City
StateOrProvince

CREATE A QUICK QUERY WITH
SIMPLE QUERY WIZARD ➤ *pp 191-194*

1. Display the Queries page of the database window, then click on New.
2. Select Simple Query Wizard and then click on OK.
3. For each field you want in the result set, choose the table or query containing the field, and then double-click on the field name.
4. Click on Next.
5. To summarize information in groups, choose Summary.
6. Click on Summary Options.
7. Select the Count Records In option to report the number of items in each group.
8. Select the operator for each field.
9. Click on OK and then on Next.
10. Enter a title for the query and click on Finish.

California Clients : Select Query

Clients	Orders
City	*
StateOrProvinc	**OrderNumber**
PostalCode	ClientID
ContactTitle	Date
PhoneNumber	ShipBy

Field:	PhoneNumber	Date
Table:	Clients	Orders
Sort:		
Show:	✓	✓
Criteria:		
or:		

SELECT RECORDS WITH QUERIES ➤ *pp 195-199*

1. Display the Queries page of the database window, and then click on New.
2. Select Design View and then click on OK.
3. Double-click on each table containing fields you want to include.
4. Click on Close.
5. Double-click on each field you want to include in the query.
6. For each field you want to sort by, click on the Sort row, and select Ascending or Descending.
7. Enter any conditions in the appropriate Criteria row.
8. Click on Query View to see the result set.
9. Click on Query View to return to Design View.
10. Save and close the query.

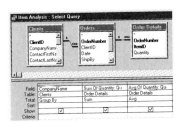

CREATE A PARAMETER QUERY ➤ *pp 201-204*

1. Create a query that includes the fields, sorts, and criteria desired.
2. In the Criteria row for each field that you want to enter as a parameter, type a prompt in square brackets.
3. If desired, use multiple parameters with the BETWEEN...AND or OR operators.
4. Run the query.
5. Enter the values desired for each parameter.

CALCULATE A VALUE WITH FIELDS ➤ *pp 204-206*

1. Create a query that includes the fields, sorts, and criteria desired.
2. In the field row for each calculated field you want to create, enter the formula for the calculation.
3. Precede the formula with a column name (header) and a colon.
4. Enclose field names in square brackets.
5. Qualify ambiguous fields with the table name in the format [Table name]![Field name].
6. Run the query.

SUMMARIZE INFORMATION ➤ *pp 206-207*

1. Create a query that includes the fields, sorts, and criteria desired.
2. Delete any fields not needed to select unique records or to be summarized.
3. Click on the Totals button to add the Total row to the grid.
4. At Group By, set those fields that will determine unique records.
5. For each field to be summarized, pull down the Total list and select the operator.
6. Run the query.

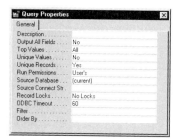

SET QUERY PROPERTIES ➤ *pp 207-208*

1. Create a query that includes the fields, sorts, and criteria desired.
2. Enter the number of records to be displayed in the Top Values box in the toolbar.
3. Click anywhere in the gray area around the field list boxes.
4. Click on the Properties button.
5. Set the query properties.

CREATE A CROSSTAB QUERY ➤ *pp 208-210*

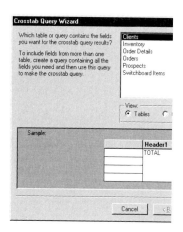

1. To create a crosstab query from fields in a related table, create and save a query that includes those fields.
2. Start a new query from the database window.
3. Choose Crosstab Query Wizard.
4. Choose the table or query to use as the basis for the crosstab, then click on Next.
5. Choose the field to use for row headings, then click on Next.
6. Choose the field to use for column headings, then click on Next.
7. Choose the fields and operators to summarize information, then click on Next.
8. Enter a name for the query and then click on Finish.

CONVERT BETWEEN FILTERS AND QUERIES ➤ *p 210*

1. Display a Filter By Form or Advanced Filter/Sort window.
2. To convert a query to a filter, choose Load From Query from the File menu and select the query. To convert the filter to a query, choose Save As Query from the File menu and enter a query name.

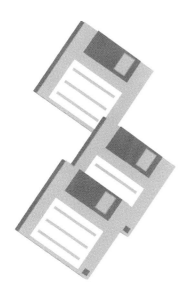

Queries are the fastest way to get information out of a database. After all, having thousands of records stored on your disk is not the reason to have a database program— doing something with the darn stuff is. Sure, you can get information using forms and reports, and you can even use filters to select which records you want to appear. But you'll get the job done much faster with queries.

WHAT'S A QUERY?

You can use a query whenever you find yourself thinking "I need to know," or when you're asking who, what, when, where, and how questions. "Who owes me money?" "What is Bob's telephone number?" "When was my fourth divorce granted?" "Where's my copy of the *Star Wars* video?" "How much do I still owe the IRS?" A query lets you see just the specific fields and records you're interested in, when you're not interested in seeing it all. You can also perform calculations on fields and summarize information in groups, and you can even group together fields from multiple tables and other queries.

The output of a query is a special datasheet called a result set, which is also known as a dynaset. A *result set* shows the results of a query: the fields you asked for and the records that meet any conditions that you establish. But it is still a datasheet of the table, so any changes you make to the information in the result set are actually made to the table.

QUICK QUERIES WITH THE SIMPLE QUERY WIZARD

The Simple Query Wizard is a way to create a query without worrying about how queries actually work. It is great even when you want to make some not-so-simple queries to summarize information.

As with other wizards, you select the fields you want to include—even from related tables—and you tell Access how you want the information presented. For example, suppose you want to analyze

The main limitation of Simple Query Wizard is that you cannot use it to select specific records, unless you create the query and then edit it in Design View.

client orders in terms of inventory. You will need to use fields from two tables, Clients and Order Details.

To create a query, click on the Queries tab of the database window, and then click on New so Access displays this dialog box:

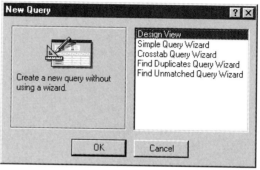

In addition to the Design View option (which lets you create a query manually in Design View) and the Simple Query Wizard, there are three other wizards that you can choose from. These other wizards are described in Table 10-1. They're relatively intuitive to use, so except for the Crosstab Query Wizard (which will be explained later in the "Creating a Crosstab Query" section), we won't bother going over them in this chapter.

Wizard	Function
Crosstab Query Wizard	Analyzes information like a spreadsheet. You select the fields to use for the row and column headings and the fields to summarize in the body of the "spreadsheet."
Find Duplicates Query Wizard	Finds records that have values in common, including duplicate records.
Find Unmatched Query Wizard	Locates records that have no matching values, such as clients who have not placed an order and thus their number is not matched in the Orders table.

Table 10.1 Additional Query Wizards

To start creating a query, click on the Simple Query Wizard option and then on OK. The first Simple Query Wizard dialog box will look very familiar: it lets you select fields from one or more tables, just as you learned in previous chapters when creating a form and report. To analyze client orders in terms of inventory, select the Clients table (in the Tables/Queries list) and then double-click on the ClientID and CompanyName fields to add them to the query. Then, select the Order Details table and add the Quantity field. After you choose the field and click on Next, Access displays a dialog box for you to choose how you want to display the records, as shown in Figure 10.1.

If you select to see all of the records, the result set lists a row for each item ordered. In our example, we're not interested in the details, just the summary by client, so click on Summary, and then on the Summary Options button so you can choose how you want the information analyzed. Note that you cannot select the Count or Field Summary Options without first choosing to summarize the data.

A dialog box appears listing the numeric and currency fields in the query—in this case, just Quantity—and the options Sum, Avg, Min, and

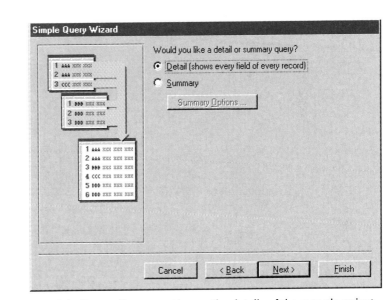

Figure 10.1 Choose if you want to see the details of the records or just summarize their data

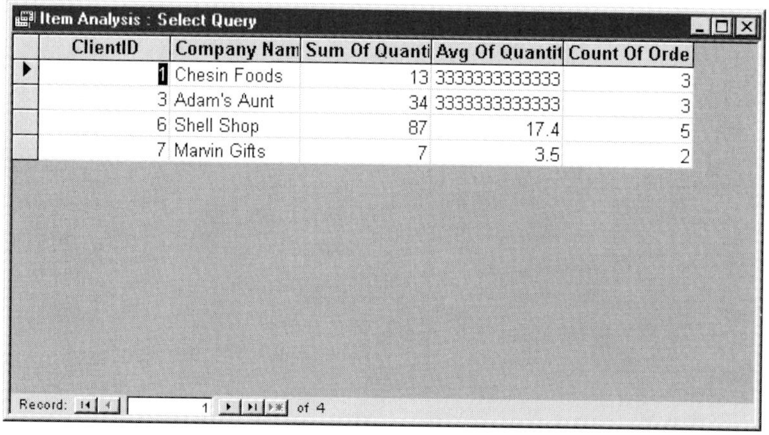

Figure 10.2 This simple query—shown in Datasheet View—contains fields from two tables

If you include a date field in the query, a Wizard dialog box appears asking how you want to group the dates. Options are Unique date/time, Day, Month, Quarter, and Year.

Max for each field. To calculate the total quantity of items ordered, click on Sum, and to average the number of items per order, click on Avg. You should also click on the Count Records In Order Details check box for a total count, and then you can click on OK to return to the Wizard dialog box. Click on Next. The final Wizard dialog box lets you enter a query title and select to display the results or the design. The results of our sample query, which we've called Item Analysis, are shown in Figure 10.2. The query results show one row for each client, reporting the total number of items ordered, the average number of items per order, and the number of orders for all invoices.

When you're done looking at the results, close the query window. You do not have to save the query, because the Wizard automatically saves it for you.

RUNNING A QUERY

As with a form or report, you can open a saved query at any time. Opening a query runs the query, showing the selected records in a result set. To run a query, follow the steps shown here.

RUNNING A QUERY step by step

1. Display the Queries page of the database window.

2. Double-click on the query name.

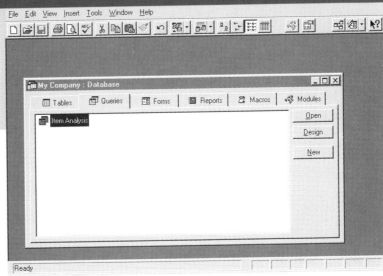

Look at the Tables/Queries page of the Options dialog box to see what default values you can set for queries.

SELECTING RECORDS WITH QUERIES

In the Simple Query Wizard dialog boxes you can choose fields and perform mathematical operations, but you can't enter criteria as you can in a filter. What if, for example, you're planning a beach vacation and you'd like to mix a little business with pleasure (or the other way around, if you're planning on deducting the trip as a business expense)? You don't want to list every client in the result set, just those in California, or New Jersey, or Florida, or wherever you're planning to go.

Rather than use the Simple Query Wizard, create the query in Design View. To do this, click on New in the Queries page of the database window, choose Design View, and then click on OK. Access displays the query window with the Show Table dialog box:

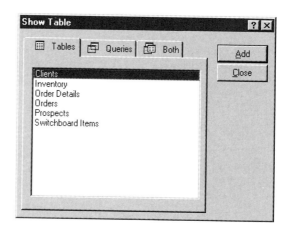

In this dialog box, you can choose the tables you want to use for the query. You can select a single table or related tables. For our example, we want to query the Clients table, so click on Clients and then on Add (or double-click on Clients), and then close the box. The query window will appear with the table, much like the Advanced Filter/Sort grid you learned about in Chapter 3. (We told you that learning about the grid would come in handy.)

Choosing Fields to Display

After you add the tables to the query window, you have to add the fields that you want to use for the query. To add a field to the grid, double-click on it or drag it to the first blank column in the field row. (You can widen the field list box to display the field's full names.) For our example, we want to display clients in a specific state, so double-click on CompanyName in the Clients table, then in the same way add the ContactLastName, the StateOrProvince, and the PhoneNumber fields (in that order). Notice that the Tables row shows the table where the field information is coming from. This will be more useful when you're using fields from related tables.

Sorting Records

You should also sort the result set in a way that makes the information more useful. To make it easier to find a specific client, for example, click in the Sort row of the CompanyName field, pull down the list, and select Ascending. Your other options are Descending and (not sorted) (the parentheses are Access's idea, not ours). This will sort the result set by client names. However, you do not have to use a sort or criteria if you want to see all of the records in their original order.

Selecting Records with Criteria

To list clients in a specific state, you need to enter a criterion. To do this, click on the Criteria row in the column for the field and type the value you want to use. For example, to list clients in California, click in the Criteria row under StateOrProvince and then type **CA**. Criteria work the same way in queries as you learned to use them for filters. (Review Chapter 3 for information on criteria.) Here's a recap:

- Enter a specific value to test for equality.
- Use operators to test for values (<,>, <=, =<. <>).
- Use AND or OR operators for compound conditions.
- Use Is Null to test for blank fields, Is Not Null for fields with contents.
- Use In to determine if the value is in a set of values.
- Use BETWEEN...AND to test for a range.
- Criteria for multiple fields are treated as an AND condition.
- Use the Or row in the grid to create OR conditions for a field or between multiple fields.

From Design View, you display the result set by clicking on either the Query View or Run Query buttons. For our sample query, Access will list the name, state, and telephone number of clients in California. Click on Query View again to return to Design View. You can always click on Query View to toggle back and forth between the design and datasheet views. (To modify an existing query, select it in the Queries page and then click on Design.)

Query View ⟶   ⟵ Run Query

Now consider the Show row. When the check box in the row (we'll call it the Show box) is checked, the field in that column of the

Filters and queries not only look alike but also can be interchanged. Refer to "Filters and Queries" later in this chapter.

SHORTCUT

Do you like the Simple Query Wizard but wish it could select specific records? Use the Wizard to create the query, then open it in Design View and add the criteria yourself.

SHORTCUT

grid will appear in the result set. Since all of the clients listed are in California, you really don't need to include the state in the result set, but you can't delete the field from the query because you need it in the grid for the criteria. To use the field for the query but not show it in the result set, deselect its Show box to remove the check mark in the Show row. If you do that and run the query, the StateOrProvince field is not shown in the result set but it is still used to limit the list by its content.

When you open a query, by the way, Access will delete all fields with the Show box deselected if they are not used for sorting, criteria, or parameters. If they are being used, Access will move the fields to the end of the grid, following the last displayed field.

If you have created the query that we've discussed, save it with the database: choose Save from the File menu, type **California Clients**, and click on OK.

Using All Fields

If you want to use all, or a majority, of the fields in a query, you don't have to bother with moving them individually. To move all of the fields to the grid, double-click on the table name on the top of the field list box to select all fields, and then drag the selection to the field row. All of the fields will be inserted, one per column. You can then select a sort order and set criteria in as many fields as required.

You can also include all of the fields by dragging the asterisk from the top of the field list into the grid. In this case, the individual fields do not appear in the table; just the name of the table and an asterisk—like Clients.*—appears in one of the columns. When you run the query, however, all of the fields appear in the result set.

You cannot designate a sort or criteria for the column using an asterisk, because it does not represent any individual field. There's a quick solution. In addition to the asterisk, drag any individual field that you want to use for a sort order or criteria, and then make your selections or entries for it. Deselect its Show box so the field will not appear twice in the result set (once from the asterisk and again from the individual column). For example, here is a query that displays all of the fields from the Clients table but only those clients from California sorted by last name.

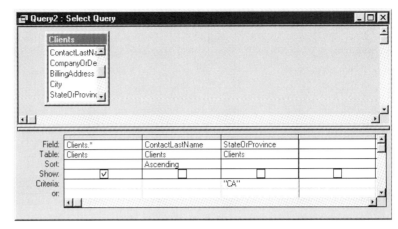

ADDING TABLES TO A QUERY

A query can include fields from more than one table, even if you only select one table originally. To add a table, follow the steps shown here.

ADDING A TABLE step by step

1. Click on the Show Table button in the toolbar.

2. Double-click on the tables you want to add.

3. Close the Show Table box.

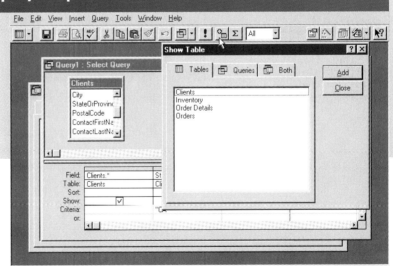

If you have already closed the query, click on California Clients in the Queries page and then click on Design. Add the Orders table. If the tables are related, Access will show a line between the related fields. For example, if you add the Orders table to the California Clients query, a line appears showing the one-to-many relationship:

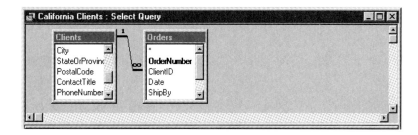

If you did not establish formal relationships, Access will relate the tables in the query if the added table contains a field name that matches the primary key in the table already there.

You can now use fields from both tables. For example, if you want to see the dates on which clients placed orders, just double-click the Date field in the Orders table.

Joining Tables

Adding tables to a query can create potential problems. For example, all of the California clients in our sample database have placed orders. But if one hadn't, and you had run the query with both the Clients and the Orders tables, the result set would have included just California clients who have placed orders, even though there is nothing in the query to make this selection. When you have related tables in the query window, Access will join the tables using only matching fields—in this case, only for California clients whose ID number is in the Orders table.

Because Access joins related tables even if you do not use fields from the child tables, only add related tables when you want to use their fields in the query. If you do not want to use fields from a child table, do not even display the table in the query window.

To avoid some of the problems caused by related tables, you can change the way the tables are joined. To do so, double-click on the join line between the tables to see a dialog box like the one shown in Figure 10.3. The first option, which is the default setting, lists only records where the joined fields match.

The second option in the dialog box will display all of the records in the parent table that meet the criteria, even if their keys are not

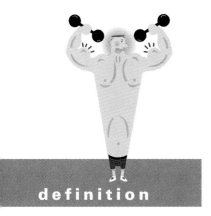

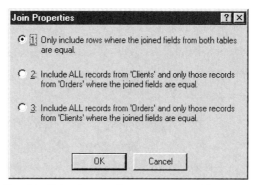

Figure 10.3 Use this dialog box to change the way tables are joined

Join: An association between fields that defines a relationship between tables.

matched in the child. If clients have not placed orders, for example, the Date column will be blank. When you choose this option and return to the query window, the join line will be pointing to the child table, which indicates this type of join. If you now run the query, the result set will list every California client, even those who have not placed an order.

If you select the third option, Access will list all of the records in the child table that meet the criteria, and only those in the parent that match. Since you have enforced referential integrity, however, the first and third options in the dialog box will have the same result set.

ALL-PURPOSE PARAMETER QUERIES

Entering specific criteria into a query really limits it. If you change your mind and decide to call on clients while vacationing on the fair beaches of New Jersey, for example, you can't just run the same query—it will always show clients in California. Instead of using specific criteria, you can enter a parameter.

As an example, you could make the California Clients query more useful by changing it so you can select the state at the time you run the query. In Design View, you have to delete any text in the Criteria row for the StateOrProvince field, and then enter a prompt such as **[Enter the State]** directly in the grid or after pressing SHIFT-F2 to see the Zoom box. (You do not have to display the Zoom box to enter long criteria—just type it in the column.) The parameter serves as a prompt, letting you

Parameter: A prompt that allows you to specify simple criteria each time you run the query.

habits & strategies

Leave the Show box selected for the parameter field. Showing the field will remind you what criteria you've entered.

know what you have to enter when you run the query, and it must be surrounded by square brackets.

When you run the modified query (either from the Query window or from the Database window), Access displays this dialog box:

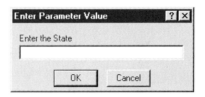

If you type **NJ** and then click on OK, Access lists clients only in New Jersey.

Using Multiple Parameters

You should strive to create queries that are as flexible as possible. Whenever you can, use parameters instead of "hard coding" the criteria into the query. This way, you can use a query as a general solution rather than a specific one. The above query, for example, can be run (opened) to locate clients in any particular state, not just the one entered in the Criteria row. Many beginning Access users forget about parameters and end up with long lists of queries that could easily be reduced to just a few.

For even greater flexibility in selecting records, use more than one parameter—as many as you need to select records. As an example, suppose you want to list clients in a specific state who have placed orders during a certain time period. You will need three parameters: the name of the desired state and a starting and ending date of orders. The query we modified above already has a parameter for the state; now enter this criteria in the Date field: **BETWEEN [Enter the starting date] AND [Enter the ending date]**.

Now when you run the query, three boxes appear. You can enter **NJ** in the first, then **1/1/96** for the starting date in the second box and **6/1/96** for the ending date in the third prompt box.

There are other ways to use two parameters in one field. The BETWEEN...AND syntax, for example, can be used to test for a numeric or currency range as well, such as BETWEEN [Enter low salary range]

AND [Enter high salary range] to list employees in a certain range of income.

You can also use multiple parameters to create an OR condition. When you run the query that includes the parameter in the StateOr-Province field, you can only enter one state abbreviation when the parameter prompt appears—you cannot type, for example, **CA or PA**. If you know you want to test for two values, you can enter a parameter like this: [Enter one state] OR [Enter the other state]. You'll see two prompts, and Access will use them for an OR condition.

Changing Parameter Order

If you run the above query, Access first requests the state and then the dates. That's because the parameters are in that order, from left to right, in the query grid. You can change the order that parameters are asked for in two ways. In the first way, you change the order of the fields in the grid by dragging their columns, just as you do in a datasheet. This also changes the order in which the fields appear in the result set. If you want to change the order in which parameters are asked for but not their order in the result set, then follow the second way and use the Parameters box.

To display the box shown here, click on the Query menu and choose Parameters:

You might also need to set the order if you use a parameter in a field that is not shown, since Access will move it to the end of the table.

Type each of the parameters in the order you want them to appear. Type the exact same thing you entered in the square brackets, but don't include the brackets. For each, pull down the Data Type list, and select the same type as the field. Then click on OK. When you run the query, the parameters will be asked for in their order in the list.

CALCULATING VALUES WITH FIELDS

So far, you've used queries to select and display data from your table. There's a lot of other information that a table can give you. This information can be calculated from the values that are stored in the table. For example, the Order Details table contains a field called Quantity, and the Inventory table has a field called Cost. Quantity is how many of the item the client orders; Cost is the price of that item. To calculate the extended price, you multiply the values in the two fields. (You'll also need to calculate the extended price to later calculate the total price of the order.)

For example, Figure 10.4 shows a query that can serve as the basis for an inventory report. It contains the ClientID field from the Clients table, the OrderNumber and Date fields from the Orders table, and the ItemID field from the Order Details table. The Inventory table is also in the query window (just below the grid so you can't see it) so its fields are available to perform the calculation of the extended price. Note that you can also sort and enter criteria in calculated columns.

To perform a calculation, you enter an *expression* (a mathematical operation) in the Field row. In our example, enter **Extended:[Order Details]![Quantity]*[Cost]** in the empty column in the Field row next

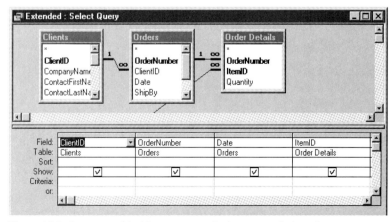

Figure 10.4 Start out with this query to calculate extended totals

to the ItemID field. The notation Extended: designates the text to use for the column heading—enter the heading followed by a colon. If you do not specify a heading, Access will create a rather cryptic one for you. Enter the field names, exactly as they are called in the table, in square brackets, and use the mathematical operators to perform the math.

If a field name is only in one of the tables, you do not have to use the table name. However, two of our tables have a field called Quantity. If you had used only the field names in this operation, Access would slap your hands and display an error reporting an ambiguous field name. We don't want to upset Access, so indicate which field to use in the notation by including the table name, an exclamation point, and then the field name, as follows: [Order Details]![Quantity]. In this case, you're using the Quantity field from the Order Details table, not from the Inventory table.

Run the query, and you see the extended cost of each item in the invoice. (When you add another field to the grid, Access automatically selects its Show box.)

Setting Properties

Access will display field values using the same format they have in the table. When it shows information from a currency field, for example, the values will appear formatted as currency in the result set. When you create a calculated field, however, you should set its properties to determine how you want it to appear.

To set the field's properties, click in any row of the calculated field, click the right mouse button, and select Properties from the shortcut menu. You can also click in the field and then on the Properties button in the toolbar. You'll see this dialog box:

You can build complex calculation expressions using built-in functions by clicking on the Build button to display the Expression Builder box. When you have time, open one of your queries and try it out.

Field Properties

General | Lookup |

Description . . . .
Format . . . .
Decimal Places . . . . .
Input Mask . . . .
Caption . . . .

Most of the properties are used for advanced functions. The Input Mask property determines the format to enter if the field contains a parameter. To set the format, pull down the Format list and select the format you want to use, then close the dialog box.

SUMMARIZING INFORMATION

The Simple Query Wizard lets you summarize information by group. You may also want to summarize information in queries that you create in Design View. For example, we just looked at a query that listed the extended amount for each item in an order. Rather than be concerned with the details, however, you may be more interested to see the total value for each order. In order to summarize information, you need to add another row to the grid and tell Access which fields to use for the group and what type of math to perform.

To add the row, click on the Totals button to display a row labeled Total. By default, all of the fields are set at Group By. If you want to calculate the total of invoices, you want to group by fields that will result in the individual orders, such as ClientID and OrderNumber, because they represent unique orders.

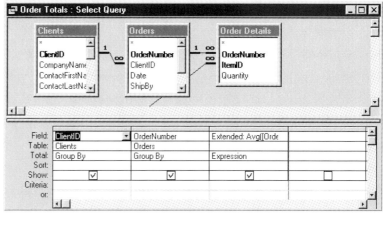

We're also no longer interested in the individual items, so you can delete the Date and the Item fields: click on the gray bar above the column to select it, and press DEL to delete it. In the fields that you're not grouping by, you designate the type of summary to create. For example, to display the total for every invoice, click in the Total row for

the calculated field, pull down the list, and select Sum. When you run the query, Access will display the total of the calculated fields for each order.

The Total list contains a number of options other than Sum. You can choose from other mathematical and statistical operations, use the Where option, or create an expression. Select Where when you want to specify a criterion to form the groups. For example, if you only want to include New Jersey clients, add the StateOrProvince field to the grid, choose Where as the operator, and enter **NJ** in the Criteria row. (When you select Where, Access automatically deselects the field's Show box.)

The Where operator determines which records to use for the groups. You may also want to determine which group results are shown. For instance, suppose you only want to list an order if its total is over $500. You do this in the Criteria row for the calculated field by entering **>500** in the Criteria row.

QUERY PROPERTIES

There are other ways to control which records or groups are reported. You may have noticed the text box in the Query toolbar with All as its selection. This is the Top Values box. By default, Access lists all of the records that meet your criteria. When you're sorting your records, however, you may only be interested in certain ones, such as the top five largest orders or the ten lowest-ranked students.

To specify a number of records to display, enter the number in the Top Values text box, or pull down the list and choose from these options:

You can also control the output using Query properties. To display the Query properties, click anywhere in the gray area around the field list boxes and click on the Properties button (or right-click and choose Properties from the shortcut menu) to see this dialog box:

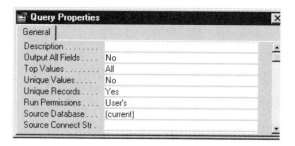

Enter a setting in the Top Values property, or select one from the list that appears.

The other two most useful properties are Unique Values and Unique Records. While no two entire records in a table should be alike, there may be a combination of fields used in a query that may result in duplicate rows in the result set. When Unique Values is set at No, Access will display all of the records, even if the values in the fields are the same. When set at Yes, only one of each row appears in the result set.

The Unique Records property is similar, but it takes into account all of the fields, even those not used in the query. When set at Yes, duplicate records are not used for the query.

We're done with the Query Properties dialog box, so you can close it now. If you created the query as we've described it, save it with the name Order Tables and then close the query window.

To show as much data as possible, set both the Unique Values and Unique Records properties at No.

CREATING A CROSSTAB QUERY

While the other query wizards are rather straightforward and intuitive, we'd like to briefly cover the Crosstab Query Wizard. A *crosstab* (a shortened form of cross tabulation) analyzes information based on two or more fields from one or more tables. For example, suppose you're interested in the ordering habits of clients. You want to see what products your clients order as well as the totals for each item. This means looking at the data in two ways, by client and by the item:

ClientID	Total Of Quant	Bananas, dried	Cider, Apple	Cider, Grape	Coffee
1	13	3		4	
3	34			12	
6	87				
7	7		4		

Stock Flow : Crosstab Query

While you can create a crosstab

query manually in Design View,

it pays to use the Crosstab

Query Wizard.

You can select up to three fields, but
too many makes the crosstab more
difficult to interpret.

Unfortunately, Crosstab Query Wizard can only use fields from one table or query and not from related tables. To use fields from related tables in a crosstab, you should first create a regular query that contains those fields. To analyze client orders, for example, let's start by creating a query in Design View with the ClientID field from the Clients table, the Quantity fields from the Order Details table, and the Item field from the Inventory table. The query window would also include the Orders table because it links the other tables. This simple query will show the item and quantity of each item for all orders.

After you create and save that query—call it something such as For The Crosstab—start a new query from the database window, choosing the Crosstab Query Wizard. The first Wizard dialog box asks what table or query you want to use for the crosstab fields. If just the tables are listed, click on the Queries option button to list the queries in the database, then click on the query you created to use for the crosstab, and then click on Next.

In the second Wizard dialog box, designate the field you want to use for the row headings. If you are analyzing client orders, for example, double-click on ClientID and then on Next. The next Wizard dialog box asks what field to use for the column headings. For our example, use the Item field to get this second dimension in the analysis.

The next Wizard dialog box asks which field to use for the summaries and the type of operator to use. It uses average by default. To total the quantity, for example, select Sum in the Function list, and make sure the Yes, include summary rows check box is enabled.

The last Wizard dialog box is the old standard—it asks for the name (we've called ours Stock Flow) and if you want to view it or show it in Design View.

Figure 10.5 shows the sample crosstab query in Design View. As you can see, a crosstab query is a special type of total query, with an additional row called Crosstab. (You'll learn about other query types in Chapter 14.)

In the Crosstab row, pull down the list that appears and designate how the field is being used. The options are Row Heading, Column Heading, Value, and Not Shown. You must have at least one row and column heading and one value field. Selecting Not Shown uses the field for sorting or criteria but does not include it in the result set. The Row

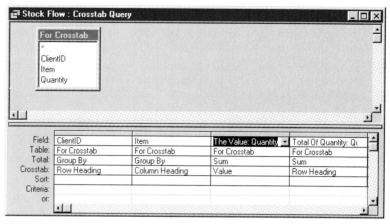

Figure 10.5 A crosstab query is a special kind of total query

Heading and Column Heading fields are used for groups, and the Value field must use a summary operator.

FILTERS AND QUERIES

Filters and queries do similar work. They both use a grid arrangement to determine what records appear and how they are sorted. Once you create one, you can quickly use it as the other. When a Filter By Form or Advanced Filter/Sort window is displayed, pull down the File menu and select one of these options:

- Save As Query saves the filter specification as a query. You can then open or change the query just as one you create from Design View.
- Load From Query lets you use the specifications from an existing query in the current filter.

SO WHAT'S NEXT?

You've been working with all of the bits and pieces of an Access database. It's now time to work with the whole thing.

CHAPTER 11

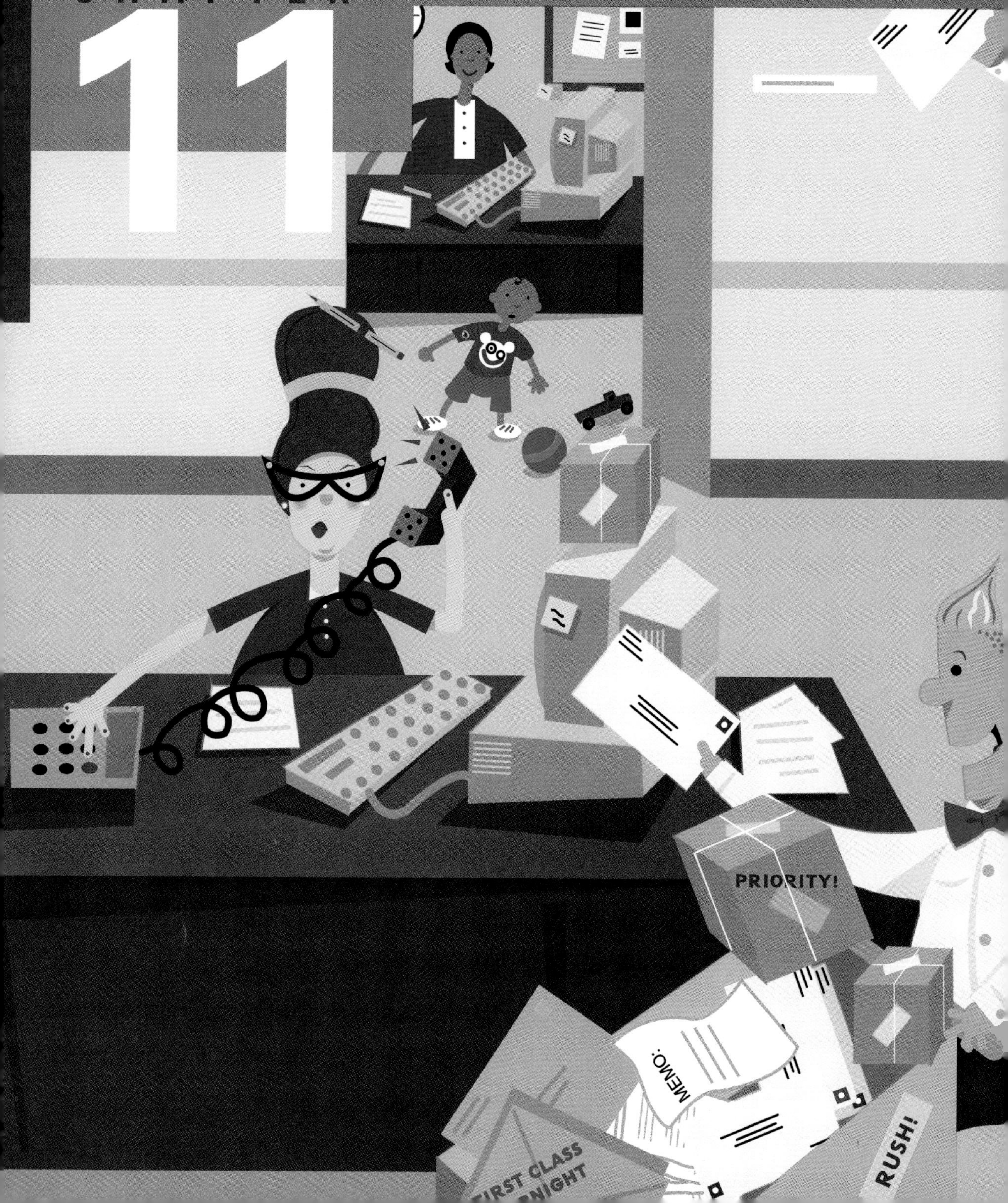

Refining Databases and Tables

FAST FORWARD

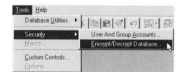

PROTECT DATA WITH PASSWORDS ➤ *pp 218-219*

1. Choose Open Database from the File menu.
2. Make certain that the Exclusive check box is selected.
3. Double-click on the database that you want to secure.
4. Pull down the Tools menu, point to Security, and click on Set Database Password.
5. In the dialog box that appears, type your secret password.
6. In the Verify box, type the same password again.
7. Click on OK.
8. To remove a password, pull down the Tools menu, point to Security, select Unset Database Password, enter the password, and then click on OK.

ENCRYPT OR DECRYPT A DATABASE ➤ *p 220*

1. Close all databases.
2. Pull down the Tools menu, point to Security, and click on Encrypt/Decrypt Database.
3. Select the database that you want to encrypt (or decrypt), and click on OK.
4. To complete encryption, enter a name and select a location where you want to store the database, and click on Save.

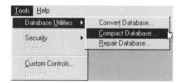

COMPACT A DATABASE ➤ *p 221*

1. Close all databases.
2. Pull down the Tools menu, point to Database Utilities, and click on Compact Database.
3. Select the database you want to compact, and click on OK.
4. Enter a name and select the location where you want to store the compacted database, and click on Save.

REPAIR DAMAGED DATABASES ➤ *pp 221-222*

1. Close all databases.
2. Pull down the Tools menu, point to Database Utilities, and click on Repair Database.
3. Select the database you want to repair, and click on Repair.
4. Click on OK to close the message box that appears.

SPLIT A DATABASE ➤ *pp 222-223*

1. Open the database.
2. Pull down the Tools menu, point to Add-ins, and click on Database Splitter.
3. Click on Split Database.
4. Type the name of a new database where you want to store the tables.
5. Click on Split.

IMPORT OBJECTS FROM OTHER DATABASES ➤ *pp 223-225*

1. Open the database you want to add objects to.
2. Pull down the File menu, point to Get External Data, and click on Import.
3. Double-click on the database containing the object you want to import.
4. Click on all of the objects you want to import.
5. If necessary, click on Options and enable the desired option.
6. Click on OK.

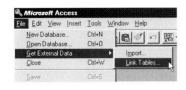

LINK A TABLE ➤ *pp 223-224*

1. Open the database to which you want to add a linked table.
2. Pull down the File menu, point to Get External Data, and click on Link Tables.
3. Double-click on the database containing the object you want to link.
4. Click on all of the tables you want to link.
5. Click on OK.

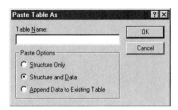

COPY AN OBJECT TO
ANOTHER DATABASE ➤ *pp 225-226*

1. Open the database containing the object you want to copy.
2. Right-click on the object and choose Copy or Cut from the shortcut menu.
3. Open the other database and display any page of the database window.
4. Right-click the mouse and click on Paste.
5. Enter an object name and select paste options, if given.
6. Click on OK.

READ DATABASE PROPERTIES ➤ *pp 226-228*

1. Open the database.
2. Click on Database Properties in the File menu.

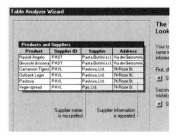

ANALYZE A TABLE ➤ *pp 228-230*

1. Open the database.
2. Pull down the Tools menu, point to Analyze, and click on Table.
3. Read the first Wizard box and click on Next.
4. Read the second Wizard box and click on Next.
5. Double-click on the table to be analyzed.
6. Select Yes, let the Wizard decide, and then click on Next.
7. Adjust the suggested layout of fields, as desired, then click on Next.
8. Confirm the selection of keys, or set new keys, and then click on Next.
9. Select to have Access create a query, then click on Finish.

ANALYZE DATABASE PERFORMANCE ➤ *pp 230-232*

1. Open the database that you want to optimize.
2. Pull down the Tools menu, point to Analyze, and click on Performance.
3. Select All in the Object Type list, click on the Select All button, and then click on OK.
4. Read each suggestion, recommendation, idea, and their suggestion notes.
5. Select all of the recommendations and suggestions you want Access to perform.
6. Click on Optimize.
7. If a warning appears regarding side effects, click on Yes to continue.
8. Enter any query or other object name that you are prompted for.
9. Read the ideas and make notes about how to implement them.
10. Close the Performance Analyzer box.
11. Implement the ideas, if desired.

We all know that it's easy to get caught up with the minutiae in life. And even though a database is only as strong as its weakest link, it pays to take a step back and get a wide-angle view. Make some time to think about security against unwanted prying eyes and net-surfers and to find ways to make your database generally more efficient. In this chapter, you'll learn how to secure your database against intrusion, how to fine-tune your database by compacting and repairing it, and how to use Access to analyze performance.

PROTECTING DATA WITH PASSWORDS

The subject of passwords can bring to mind the cheap plastic decoder rings of childhood, invisible ink, and Agent Maxwell Smart speaking into his shoe. Data security used to be easy: you locked your file cabinet and hired a snarling dog or an equally snarling but less sociable security guard. Then along came computers and hackers, and security became a science on par with quantum physics.

Passwords, like locks on doors and windows, can only protect you from the casual thief. Access lets you set two types of passwords. What's imaginatively called the *database password* controls who can open a database. A more complex type of password, called the *security account password*, controls users when they log on to a network workgroup. Security account passwords, and the user-level security that they provide, is best left to database or network administrators who have the time for that nonsense. They can use something called the Security Wizard from the Tools menu, although even they shouldn't run the wizard until they've taken some other steps that network administrators like to keep to themselves.

CAUTION

Don't forget your password—you'll lock yourself out without it. If you don't trust your memory, write down the password and store it in your sock drawer.

Now for the rest of us. To set a database password, follow the steps shown below. Keep in mind that passwords are case-sensitive, so keep an eye on the CAPS LOCK key. As you type your password, only a series of asterisks will appear, protecting you from prying eyes. (Talk about paranoid.)

SETTING A PASSWORD step by step

1. Choose Open Database from the File menu.

2. Make certain that the Exclusive check box is selected, then double-click on the database that you want to secure.

3. Pull down the Tools menu, point to Security, and click on Set Database Password.

4. In the dialog box that appears, type your secret password.

5. In the Verify box, type the same password again, and then click on OK.

You should not use a database password if you are planning on synchronizing a replica database. You won't be able to synchronize it.

Now whenever you, or anyone else, opens the database, a dialog box will appear asking for the password. Type the secret password—using the same case (upper/lower) with which you created it—and then click on OK.

When you get tired of typing the password every time you open the database, then remove it. To do so, open the database (of course, you'll have to enter the password to open it), then pull down the Tools menu, point to Security, and select Unset Database Password—you'll only see this option if you're using a password. Type the password, and click on OK.

definition

Encrypt: To make indecipherable to every program except Access.

The Encrypt/Decrypt option can be found in the Security menu only when no database is open.

CAUTION

If you encrypt a database to a copy, you will actually have two sets of the same information. Be careful that you, or someone else, knows which database to use.

ENCRYPTING A DATABASE

Psst. Over here, in the shadows. Ormay ecretsay tuffsay. Pass it around.

There's one major flaw with database passwords. You don't necessarily have to open a database to see what's in it. You can open the database into most word processing programs, for example. You'll have to slosh through thousands of characters of garbage, but eventually you'll be able to read exactly what's in the tables. There are even special programs that are designed to extract information from the database and to convert it to some other form. Bill Gates must have owned one of those decoder rings as a child, though, because he lets us encrypt the database.

Encrypting sounds very protective, but it is unfortunately rather ho-hum. While no one will be able to read the table information with a word processing program, everyone who has Access can get into it as easily as you can. So encryption, by itself, is practically useless. You have to both encrypt the database and use a password for any sort of real protection.

To encrypt a database, close any database that you're working on, but remain in Access. If you're on a network, call around and make sure no one else is using the database. If people are using the database, tell them to close it, or wait until they're done. Then pull down the Tools menu, point to Security, and then click on Encrypt/Decrypt Database. In the dialog box that appears, select the database that you want to encrypt, and then click on OK. In the next dialog box that appears, enter a name and select where you want to store the database, and then select Save.

If you use the same name and location as the original (non-encrypted) database, Access will replace it with the encrypted version. If you use a different name or location, Access makes an encrypted copy of your database. In either case, during the process you'll need enough hard disk space to store the original file and the encrypted copy. You decrypt a database following the exact same steps as for encrypting a database.

Just remember, encrypting the database by itself does not provide any protection against a thief who also has Access.

When you encrypt a database, Access also compacts it.

The Database Utilities option can be found in the Tools menu only when no database is open.

COMPACTING A DATABASE

Database files can be very large. If you've already got a lot of stuff on your hard disk, there might not be enough space to store all of the database in one piece. If this happens, Windows saves the bits and pieces of the database wherever it can. When you open the database, Windows collects the bits and pieces together. The situation gets worse as you add and delete records, tables, and other objects. So after a time, you've got database scattered all over the hard-disk landscape. Compacting (also known as defragmentation) draws all of the pieces together and stores them all, or as much as possible, in one place. This makes Access run a little faster and you a little happier.

Here's how to compact a database. Close all databases (but remain in Access), select Database Utilities from the Tools menu, and click on Compact Database. In the dialog box that appears, select the database you want to compact, and then click on OK. Next, enter the name and select the location where you want to store the compacted file. As with encrypting, you can give the same name and location as the original, or you can use a different name or location to make a compacted copy. If you do want to compact it to the same name, make a copy of it first in another location.

Compacting a database has a nice side benefit if you use an AutoNumber field. Normally, Access doesn't recycle AutoNumber values. If you delete a record, its number will not be assigned to a new record. Compacting changes this, to a degree. If you've deleted records from the end of a table, Access will reset the AutoNumber value to one higher than the last undeleted record, so new records begin AutoNumbering from that point.

DAMAGE CONTROL (OR, REPORT SCOTTIE!)

Microsoft Access builds a pretty solid database, but things can still go wrong. During all of the bumping and grinding of your hard disk, something can happen to the database file as it is etched into electrons. When Access opens, compacts, encrypts, or decrypts a database, it will usually report if it detects any problem with the database and will ask if you want to repair it. But this self-diagnosis doesn't always work. If your database acts as strange as a Democrat in the Rush Limbaugh

If the database cannot be repaired, try using a backup copy. If that doesn't work, call for support!

room of the Union League, then try repairing it yourself before spending money on technical support.

Close all databases, choose Database Utilities from the Tools menu, and then click on Repair Database. Select the database you want to repair and then click on Repair. A message box will report that the repair was successful. Click on OK and then test the database.

SPLITTING A DATABASE

The critical part of your database is the information in the tables. Forms, reports, queries, macros, and modules are the icing on top of the biscotti. The people who use your database don't necessarily need to use, or want to use, the same forms, reports, or queries. If everyone stored their own personalized forms and reports in the database, your database window would be cluttered like the Champs Elysées after Bastille Day.

You can let everyone have their own forms and reports by storing the tables in a separate database. This way, each user can modify his or her own objects without changing the interface of another.

Here's how. First make a backup copy of the database just in case, then open the database, pull down the Tools menu, and point to Add-ins to see these options:

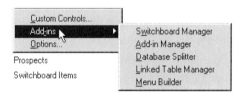

Click on Database Splitter to see the first of two Wizard boxes. This box just tells you what the splitter does and that it may take a long time. Click on Split Database. In the dialog box that appears, type the name of a new database where you want to store the *tables* and then click on Split.

Access does its thing and then displays a message that the database has been split. Click OK to remove the message. In the database window, you'll see arrows pointing to the tables to indicate that they are linked:

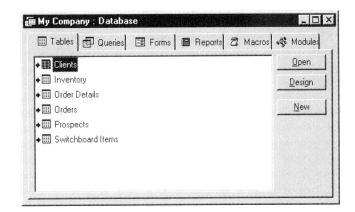

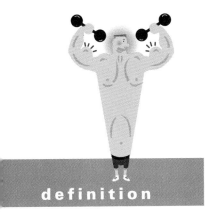

Linked: *A connection that allows one database to access tables stored in another database.*

If you need to transport the database on a floppy disk, copy both the one containing the tables and the one with the forms, reports, and other objects. If you just copy the original database, where will it get its information from?

You use the database exactly the same as before. Adding, editing, or deleting records changes the tables, just as before, except that the tables are actually part of a different database.

If you want to link the tables with another database, so that you can create a different set of forms or reports, use the Get External Data command that you will learn about next. You would also use that command if you want to unsplit the databases, placing the tables back with the forms and other objects.

USING OBJECTS FROM OTHER DATABASES

Recycling is admirable. It can save the environment and save time, and those logos are way cool. You can also save time by recycling tables, forms, reports, and other database objects. For instance, suppose you spend megatime creating a perfect database. There's a table—or some other object—in it that you'd like to use in whole or part in another database. Why re-create it, when you can just borrow it?

The Get External Data command lets you import any part of a database or create a link to a database table. Open the database you want to add objects to, then pull down the File menu and point to Get External Data. You have two choices:

- If you want to copy the object from one database to another, click on Import.
- If you want to create a link to the table, click on Link Tables.

You can also import or link tables by selecting Import Table Wizard or Link Table Wizard from the New Table dialog box.

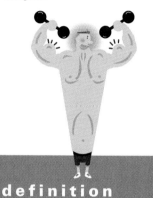

definition

Import: *To make a copy of a database object in another database.*

SHORTCUT

You can choose Import and Link Tables from the shortcut menu that appears when you click the right mouse button in the database window when no object is selected.

In the dialog box that appears, double-click on the database containing the object you want to import or link. A database window appears where you select the object itself, as in Figure 11.1. If you are linking a table, the window only contains the Tables page.

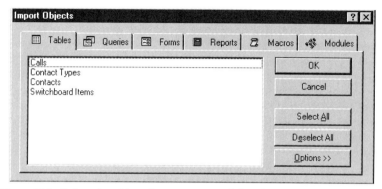

Figure 11.1 Select the object that you want to link or import

Now click on as many of the objects as you want to import or link. Clicking on one object does not remove the highlight from another. To deselect an object, click on it again. You can also use the Select All and Deselect All buttons. Before actually importing any object, you might want to check out your options. Clicking on the Options button expands the dialog box to show these choices (the options do not appear if you are linking a table):

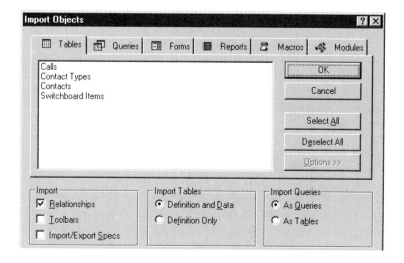

The options in the Import section let you also import relationships between tables, any custom toolbars that you've created, and specifications for importing and exporting objects. In the Import Tables section, choose to import the definition and the data or just the definition alone. Select just the definition when you want to create a new table using the same specifications but without the information. In the Import Queries section, select to import the queries as queries or as tables. Importing a query as a table is a good way to create a table using fields from related tables in the other database.

Once you've selected the object and the options, click on OK. The objects will be added to the appropriate pages of the database window. If you're linking tables, click on Link, and the tables appear in the Tables page of the database window.

Copying Objects

The Get External Data command brings objects into the open database. You can go the other way around—from the open database to another—and you can make a copy of an object in its own database.

Click on the object you want to copy in the database window, then choose Save As/Export from the File menu to see this dialog box:

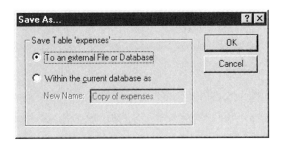

To make a copy of an object in the same database, click on Within the current database as, type the new object name in the text box, and click on OK. To copy the object to another Access database, click on To an external File or Database, and then click on OK. In the dialog box that appears, select the Access database you want to insert the copy into, and then click on Export. Next, enter a name for the object, if you want to rename it, and then click on OK.

You can also use the Clipboard to copy objects, using either the Cut, Copy, and Paste buttons on the toolbar, or the shortcut menu that

appears when you click the right mouse button. For example, to copy an object, click on it in the database window and then click on the Copy button. This is a pain, because you then have to open the other database, and click on the Paste button. But it does offer one advantage: if you copy a table, you'll see this dialog box when you choose Paste:

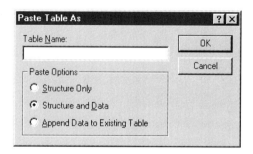

You can choose to paste just the structure of the table (its field definitions), or the structure and the data. If you want to append the information to another table having the same structure, type the name of the existing table and select Append Data to Existing Table. (If you copied an object other than a table, a box will appear for you to enter a new name.)

Unsplitting a Database

If you split a database and then change your mind, you can unsplit it. Open the database that contains the forms, reports, and other objects, and display the Tables page. Delete all of the linked objects (the ones with the arrow pointing to them) by right-clicking on the object and choosing Delete from the shortcut menu. Next, point to Get External Data in the File menu and select Import to import the tables from the database you created with the Database Splitter.

DATABASE PROPERTIES

Every object is associated with a series of properties that describe the object and give you information about it. After you open a database, select Database Properties from the File menu. You'll see a dialog box with five pages, as shown in Figure 11.2. Some of the information on the pages is redundant, and some of it is nice but relatively useless. So we'll just recap what you'll find.

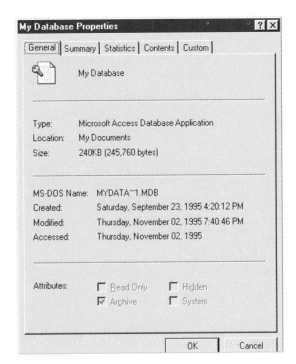

Figure 11.2 Every object is associated with this series of properties

The General page contains the name, type, location, size, and file attributes of the database, as well as its MS-DOS name and the date and time the database was created, last modified, and last accessed. The MS-DOS name is useful if you have to work with the database file under DOS and not Windows.

The Summary page lists the title, subject, author, manager, company, category, keywords, and comments. You can use the information on this page to locate databases.

The Statistics page shows the date and time the database was created, last modified, accessed, and printed. It also shows who last saved the database, the revision number, and total editing time. Revision Number reports how many times the database has been saved, even if you did not make any changes to it. Total Editing Time shows the length of the editing session, or how long the file was open even if you did not edit it, as long as you saved it. Interesting, potentially useful, even if you have to stretch.

The Contents page lists the tables, queries, forms, reports, macros, and modules in the database. The same thing you see when looking at the database window, just all together in a list format.

The Custom page lets you define your own properties—a rather advanced function for database gurus.

TABLE ANALYZER

Serious database people worry all the time if their tables are normalized. They're not concerned about IQ, social behavior, or the normal stuff that we humans care about. Normalization is a series of rules to avoid duplicated information, mistakes, and problems, and it deserves serious consideration at a certain level.

upgrade note

Table Analyzer and Performance Analyzer are new features! Use Table Analyzer if you want to normalize your database to avoid errors. Use Performance Analyzer to speed up database operations and create effective database management systems.

We're really too busy to worry about normalization, but we can take some quick steps to check the health of tables. Table Analyzer looks at a table to help fix one common mistake made by entry-level database creators: they make a table that contains duplicate information, which really should be divided into two or more related tables. The Analyzer Wizard isn't 100 percent automatic, and it needs a little help and input from you, but you can't mess anything up. It never changes your table, it just creates new ones that you can use in its place.

Open the database containing the table you want to check, then pull down the Tools menu, point to Analyze, and click on Table. The first Wizard box is purely FYI, letting you see examples of how duplicated information wastes space and can result in errors. Click on Next for another FYI box. This time, you can read how dividing the tables into two or more tables can help. Click on Next. Select the table that you want to analyze; at this point, you can also opt to deselect the Show introductory pages option for the next time you run the Wizard. After you select the table, click on Next. You now have two choices as to how your fields are arranged in the table:

- Yes, let the Wizard decide.
- No, I want to decide.

Make your selection and then click on Next.

If you choose to make the decision yourself, a box will appear so you can create additional tables and move fields around as you want. It's not unlike the other choice, to have Access do it for you, so we'll look at that option in detail.

If you choose to let the Wizard decide, Access spends a moment performing an analysis. If no corrections are needed, Access recommends not splitting the table. If corrections are needed, Access shows a suggested table layout, like the one shown in Figure 11.3. If you do not like the layout, drag fields from one table to another. You can also select buttons to rename the table, undo your action, and display tips. When you're done, click on Next. Here, you are asked to confirm the keys. The Wizard asks if the boldface fields uniquely identify the

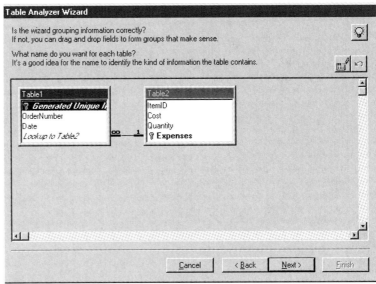

Figure 11.3 The Table Analyzer Wizard shows a suggested layout to improve your table

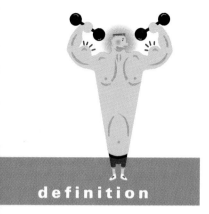

Optimize: Adjust parts of the database to achieve optimal performance.

records. You can use the buttons to set a key or have Access add a key for you. When you're happy, click on Next.

The final Wizard box asks if it should create a query that looks like the original table. Keep in mind that if it creates a whole new set of tables, leaving your original unchanged, then all of your forms, reports, and queries will still look for fields in the original table. If you tell the Wizard to create a query for you, it will rename the original table, so forms, reports, and other queries get information from the new query instead. You won't have to modify the other objects, because they are fooled into thinking they're still working with the original table.

PERFORMANCE ANALYZER

On some computers Access can run a little slow. We don't think even Microsoft would mind admitting that. Getting Access to run faster might mean adding memory or fine-tuning the Windows environment. If you don't have the money or the fortitude for these solutions, then try to optimize the database. This too can be daunting, but you're not entirely on your own.

Open the database that you want to optimize, point to Analyze in the Tools menu, and then click on Performance. You'll see a dialog box like the one in Figure 11.4.

Figure 11.4 Choose the objects that you want Access to analyze

SHORTCUT

To check the entire database, select All in the Object Type list, click on the Select All button, and then click on OK.

You have to select which objects you want Access to check. Use the Object Type list to pick the type of object, and then click on each specific object in the Object Name list. You can select any combination of objects, combining different types in the same analysis. When you've selected the desired objects, click on OK.

Access checks the objects and then displays a dialog box like the one in Figure 11.5, showing some ways to optimize the database. Icons next to each item indicate a recommendation (something you should definitely consider), a suggestion (something you should probably consider), or an idea (something to consider). Click on each suggestion to read more about it in the Suggestion Notes box.

To have Access perform a recommended or suggested change, click on the Optimize button—it will become active when you point to a recommendation or suggestion. If optimizing will create any side effects, a dialog box appears asking if you want to continue. Click on No, and read the suggestion notes to first make sure you understand the side effects. Then, if desired, click on Optimize to continue. You

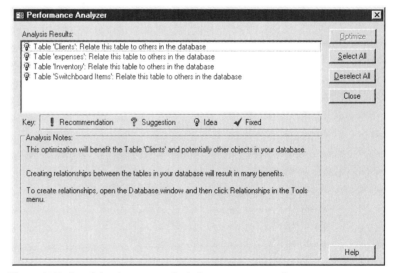

Figure 11.5 Read the Access analysis for ways you can improve your database

To put an idea into play, click on it, read the notes, and then do it yourself.

may be asked to enter the name of queries or other objects that Access creates. When it is done, Access places a check mark next to each of the items that it performed, and you can close the Performance Analyzer dialog box.

SO WHAT'S NEXT?

Use what you've learned in this book to create and manage your databases. If you run into trouble, have questions, or just forget how to do something, go back to the chapter and refresh your memory. Whenever possible, take advantage of Access Wizards and other automated features—such as AutoFormat and Format Painter—to save yourself time.

APPENDIX A

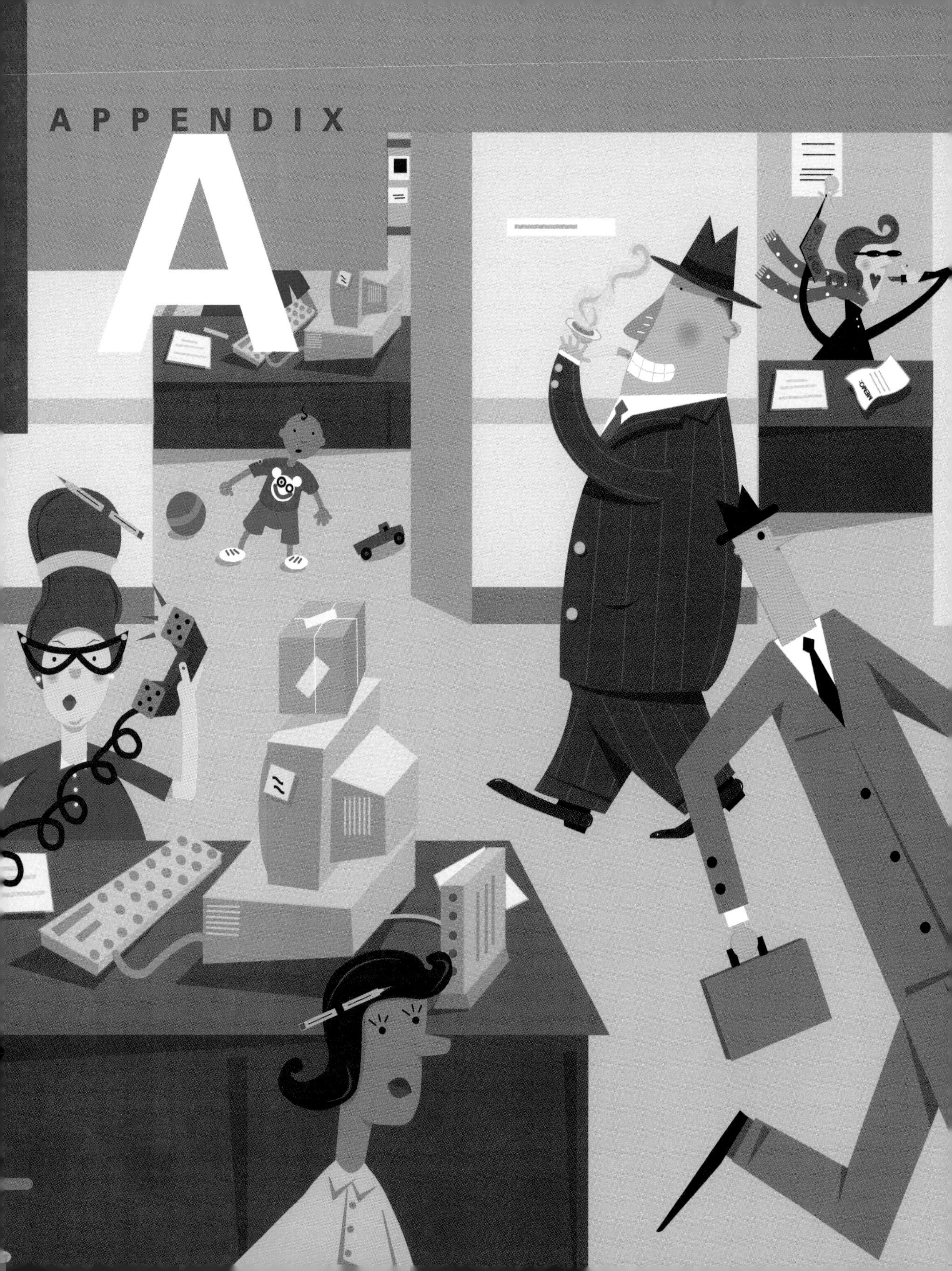

Installing Access for Windows 95

If you need to install Access on your computer, or change the way it is installed, this appendix will take through the process. You can install all or just part of Access, depending on which features you'll want to use and how much disk space you have available.

INSTALLING ACCESS

With Windows 95 up and running, insert the first Access floppy disk into your disk drive, or insert the CD-ROM into its drive. Close any open application and then run the program SETUP.EXE. To run a program, click on Start in the Taskbar and then on Run to see this dialog box:

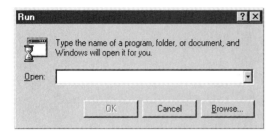

Type the path where the program SETUP.EXE can be found, such as A:\SETUP.EXE or D:\SETUP.EXE, and then click on OK. In a few moments you'll see the Access welcome screen that contains some license information. Click on Continue to be prompted to enter your name and the name of your organization. If you've already installed a Microsoft application, this information may already be filled in for you. When the box is complete, click on OK. Access will ask you to confirm the information—click on OK if it is, or click on Change and correct it if not.

The next dialog box shows you the product ID number of your copy of Access. You'll need the number to get telephone support, so write it down and store the number some place safe. You can also get the same number by choosing About Microsoft Access from the Help menu once you start Access. Click on OK to see a dialog box asking you to confirm the folder where Microsoft Office files—of which Access is a part—will be stored. When you click on OK a dialog box will appear asking you to confirm where Access will be stored. Click on OK to accept the default folder to see the options shown in Figure A.1. You now have to choose the type of setup you want to perform.

Typical installs almost every part of Access except for Developer Tools, online help about programming, and two of the three sample databases. Use this option if you have at least 33MB of free disk space, do not want to learn about Visual Basic programming, and do not plan on using some of the more sophisticated features of Access. The Developer Tools, for example, are required to use the Expression Building, Chart Wizard, and Subform/Subreport Wizard.

Compact installs just the basics of Access that you'll need for everyday work. It won't install any of the sample databases and some of the files you'll need for more advanced functions. Still, it is a good choice if you are very short on disk space since only 14.8MB are required. You can always later rerun Setup to install those features you find you really must have.

Custom lets you pick and choose what parts of Access to install. Use this option if you want to install everything, or if you want to install something between Typical and Compact. A dialog box will appear where you can select options, as shown in Figure A.2. A white-enabled check box means that all of the

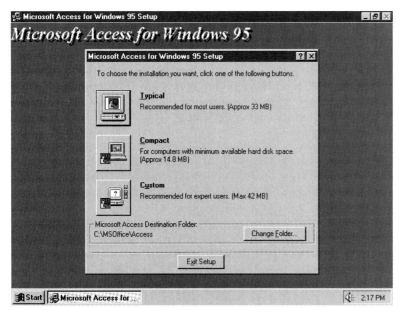

Figure A.1 Choose the type of setup you want to perform based on the features you want to use and the amount of disk space you have available

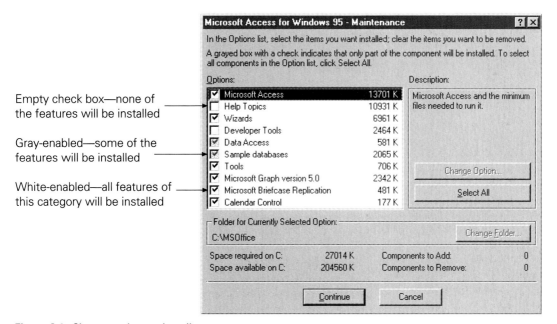

Empty check box—none of the features will be installed

Gray-enabled—some of the features will be installed

White-enabled—all features of this category will be installed

Figure A.2 Choose options to install

features in that category will be installed. A gray-enabled box means that only some features will be installed. Of course, an empty check box means that none of the features will be installed.

Click on the Select All button to install everything, or click on individual boxes to select or unselect the feature. Some of the boxes represent several related features. To pick and choose which of the features to install, click on the box and then on the Change Option button. In the dialog box that appears, select or unselect specific features, and then click on OK. Be sure to install the Developer Tools if you want to learn everything covered in this book. When you're done, click on Continue.

If you are installing Access as part of Microsoft Office, your choices will be similar to those discussed here. If you choose Typical, you'll install the basic parts of the Office suite. To install the Developer Tools, or just selected parts of Office, choose the Custom option.

Setup will now do its thing and install Access on your computer. If you're using floppy disks, you'll be prompted when to insert another disk into the drive. You won't have to worry about this if you're using a CD-ROM.

Once Access is installed, a message appears reporting that your system is being updated. During this process, Setup installs information in the system registry. Depending on your computer, this procedure can take several minutes, and for times it may even appear that nothing is happening. Just be patient and wait until you see a dialog box reporting that Access has been successfully installed. Click on OK to remove the box, and then enjoy Access for Windows 95.

ADDING OR REMOVING INSTALLED FEATURES

After you install Access you may later need to add more features, or remove some that you've already installed. Perhaps you performed a Compact installation, and then find that you need some of the sample files or other features not installed as part of that option. If you're running out of disk space, you might decide to remove the sample files or some other features that you really do not need.

To modify your installation, run the Setup program again. Since Access is already installed, you'll see the dialog box shown in Figure A.3. Click on the Add/Remove button to add or remove specific parts of Access.

The Reinstall option will set up all of the same files you last installed. Use this option if you accidentally deleted some part of Access, or if Access is not behaving correctly.

If you want to remove Access entirely from your system, click on the Remove All button.

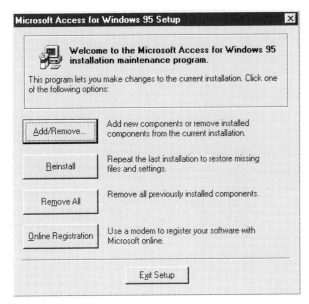

Figure A.3 Modify your Access setup by running the Setup program

APPENDIX B

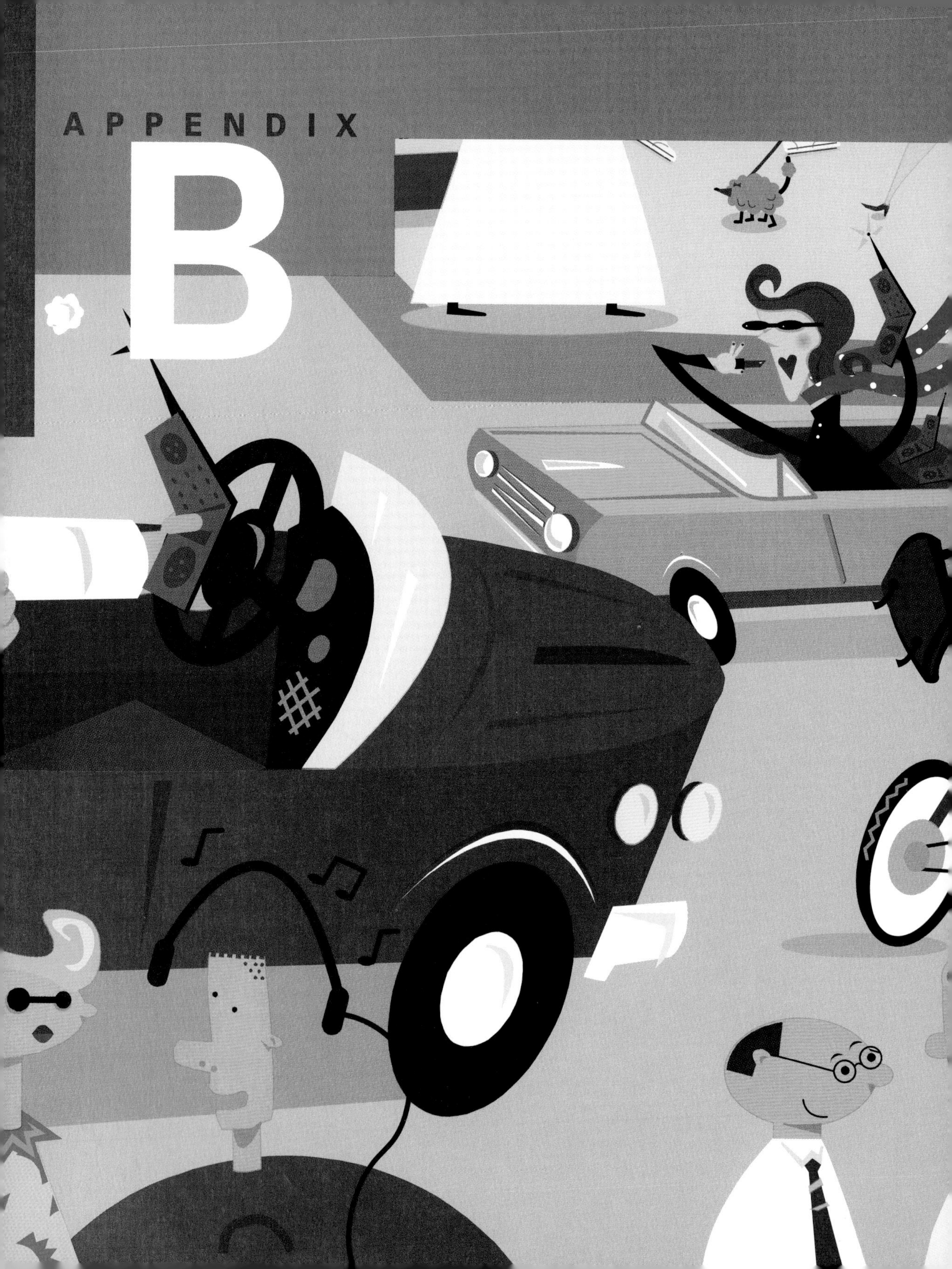

The Basics of
Windows 95

This book assumes that you've already learned the basics of Windows 95, and have perhaps read Ron Mansfield's, *Windows 95 for Busy People* (Osborne/McGraw-Hill, 1996). But if you haven't, this appendix should help you get started.

All of Microsoft's Office 95 programs (Word, Excel, PowerPoint, Schedule +, and Access) were especially designed to take advantage of the new Windows 95 operating system. If you know your way around Windows 95, you have a leg up on getting the most out of these and many other programs.

THE DESKTOP

Windows 95 starts when you turn on your computer. You don't need to type anything first, but you might be asked for a password once or twice. If you don't know one of the passwords, try pressing the ESC key (you should be able to use Windows but you might not have access to your network or to e-mail; so if passwords are required, you should contact your network administrator to set one up). When Windows 95 starts, it displays a screen called the *desktop*. Figure B.1 shows a typical Windows 95 desktop. Yours might look different. That's perfectly OK.

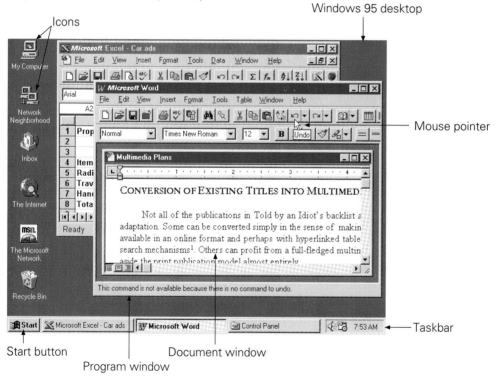

Figure B.1   A typical Windows 95 desktop

The desktop contains small pictures of items like disk drives, a recycle bin, and so on. These little pictures are called *icons*. At the bottom of the Windows 95 desktop you'll probably see the Taskbar, which will be discussed later in this appendix. Windows 95 also displays *windows*. These windows are the spaces in which you do your work. *Program windows* contain programs (like Word, or Access, or whatever) and can also contain other windows, often called *document windows* or *child windows*. So, for example, you might have a Word window on your desktop with one or more word processing document windows inside it. Any time you double-click a folder icon (or an icon representing a disk drive), it will open up as a window on the screen (and a button on the Taskbar), showing the contents of the folder (or drive).

MOUSE BASICS

You use the mouse to point to objects on the desktop. (Incidentally, some computers have trackballs or other pointing devices, but all of these devices share some common characteristics: each has at least two buttons, and each lets you point to things.) As you move the mouse or other pointing device, a corresponding *pointer* moves on the desktop. Sometimes the shape of the pointer changes to give you a clue about what you can do next, because what you can do depends on what you're pointing to.

You can also make choices with the mouse (such as choosing a menu option), and you can use it to move and resize objects. You do this by pointing to something and clicking on it, which usually selects the object or causes something to happen. *Clicking* is accomplished by pressing and releasing a mouse button. *Double-clicking* is the act of pressing and releasing a mouse button twice in rapid succession. *Dragging* is the act of clicking on an object (a window, an icon, or whatever) and moving your mouse while holding down the button.

Most computer pointing devices (mice, trackballs, and so on) have two buttons. If the buttons are side by side, and if you have not modified Windows 95's default mouse settings, you will use the left button for clicking to select things and initiate most actions. You will also use the left button to drag objects around on the desktop and to change the size and shape of things. (Lefties who like to customize their environments—I'm a lefty myself, but more of the coping-with-a-righty-world type—can switch the functions of the right and left mouse buttons.)

Windows 95 makes extensive use of the right button as well. Clicking the right button (also called *right-clicking*) on almost any screen element will pop up a *shortcut menu* full of useful options. For example, you can change the appearance of your desktop by right-clicking just about anywhere on the desktop and choosing Properties from the menu that pops up.

There is one more mouse technique worth mentioning. It is called *hovering*. Frequently, if you slide the mouse pointer over an object and leave it there for a second, a little message called a *tool tip* will pop up that will tell you something about the object. In Figure B.1, for example, Word is telling you that the button under the mouse pointer is for activating the Undo feature.

THE TASKBAR

The Taskbar lets you easily run programs and switch from window to window. (If you don't see the Taskbar at the bottom of the desktop, slide your mouse pointer down to the bottom of the screen. The Taskbar should appear.) On the left end of the Taskbar you will always see the Start button. If you have opened windows or started programs (or if Windows has started them for you), your Taskbar will also contain other buttons. See "Taskbar Tips," later, for an explanation of how these buttons work.

The Start Menu

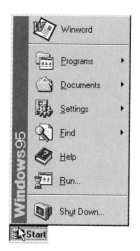

Let's begin with a look at the Start button and the Start menu that is displayed when you click on it. This is the menu from which you start programs, change Windows settings, retrieve recently used documents, find "lost" files, and get Windows 95 help. You point to items in the Start menu to choose them.

Everyone's Start menu looks a little different, particularly when you scratch the surface. (You can also add shortcuts to programs to the Start menu, such as the Winword item at the top of my menu, shown here.) The Start menu often reveals additional levels of menus called *submenus*. Let's look at the primary Start menu choices.

Programs

Roughly equivalent to the old Program Manager program groups in earlier versions of Windows, the Programs item on the Start menu pops up a submenu of programs and special Start menu folders. The folders themselves open sub-submenus, and so on. You can run any properly installed program in Windows 95 by clicking on the Start button, then clicking on the Programs choice in the Start menu, and then clicking on the desired program (or perhaps on a folder and then on a program in the folder).

Documents

The Start menu remembers the last 15 documents you've opened and displays their names in the Documents menu. (However, be forewarned that programs designed prior to Windows 95 often fail to add documents to the Documents menu.) When you want to work with a recently used document again, click on its name in the Documents menu. The document will appear on your screen in the program in which it was created. If the program is not already running, Windows 95 will launch it for you automatically.

Settings

To change the various settings for your computer, such as the way the Start menu looks or how your screen saver works, choose Settings from the Start menu and then choose Control Panel from the Settings submenu. From the resulting Control Panel window, a part of which is shown here, you can exercise centralized control over all of your computer's settings.

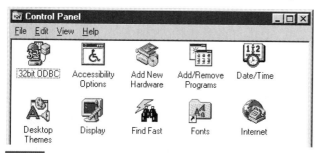

You'll need to consult online help and perhaps read a book like *Windows 95 for Busy People* to learn more about the thousands of possible setting changes.

Find

Windows 95's Find feature can be an invaluable aid for digging up files that seem to be lost in the system. To search for a file, choose Find from the Start menu and then choose Files or Folders. In the dialog box that appears, type a filename or part of one in the Named box and press ENTER or click on Find Now.

Help

Stuck? Not sure what to do? You can always consult Windows Help. To do so, choose Help from the Start menu. (If you're doing this for the first time, Windows will tell you that it's setting up Help.) In the Help Topics dialog box that appears (see Figure B.2), click on a topic from the expandable Contents list or click on the Index tab, type a key word in the first box, and choose a topic from the index list in the second box.

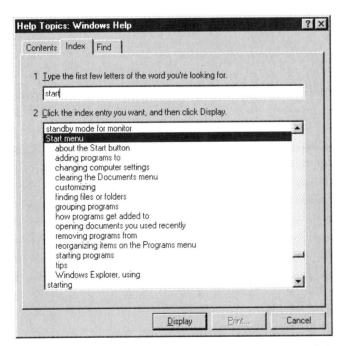

Figure B.2 Choose a topic or subtopic from the Help Topics dialog box

In most programs, if you're not sure what a button or other screen element does, you can hover the mouse pointer over it for a moment and a tool tip will appear, naming or explaining the object.

Also, in a dialog box, you can click on the What's This? button (a question mark) in the top-right corner and then click on the item in the dialog box that you want more information on. A brief explanation should pop up.

Run

Any time you know the name of a program file (although sometimes you also have to know the "path" of the folders on the hard disk that leads to the program), you can choose Run from the Start menu, type the name (or path and name) in the box, and press ENTER to run the program. It's usually easier, though, to start the program from the Start menu or one of its submenus.

Shut Down

When you want to turn off your computer, first shut down Windows 95. To do so, choose Shut Down from the Start menu. Click on Yes when asked if you want to shut down the computer. Wait until Windows tells you it's OK to turn off the computer, and then turn it off.

Taskbar Tips

Every time you start a program or open or minimize some types of windows, the program or window gets its own button on the Taskbar.

This makes it easy to switch to a program that is already running, to make a particular window active, or to maximize a window. All you have to do is click on the appropriate button on the Taskbar. When a button looks depressed (pushed in), it means that the task represented by the button is the active one, and its window will appear "in front of" the other windows.

If the Taskbar gets too crowded, you can point to its top edge and drag it so that it gets taller. You can also move the Taskbar to any side of the screen (top, bottom, left, or right) by clicking on any part of the Taskbar that is not a button and dragging. When the Taskbar is on the left or right side, you can drag its inner edge to set it to any width, up to half the width of the screen.

THE MY COMPUTER ICON

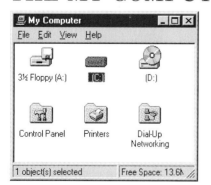

One way to explore the files and programs on your computer is to double-click on the My Computer icon. In general, double-clicking on an icon opens it, runs the program it represents, or runs the program in which the document it represents was created. If the icon is a folder or a special icon such as My Computer, it will open into a window and display its contents, which will also appear as icons. Some of these icons might represent programs, and others might represent folders or other special icons.

The My Computer window contains icons that represent your hard disk drive, floppy disk drives, and CD-ROM drive (if applicable), as well as icons for your printers, for dial-up networking, and for the Control Panel.

Double-click on the hard disk drive icon to see the contents of the hard disk. The icon opens into a window that shows folders and other icons. Double-click on any folder to see its contents. Repeat as often as necessary. You can go back up a folder level by pressing Backspace.

THE NETWORK NEIGHBORHOOD ICON

If your computer is connected to a network, you will see a Network Neighborhood icon on the desktop. Double-clicking on it will show you a list of the remote computers, disk drives, and folders that you can access.

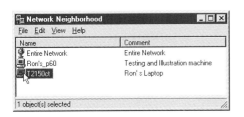

You might need to know the appropriate passwords to access some of the information on the network, and you might be limited in what you can do with files and folders on the network. For example, the owners of some files might let you read the files but not change them. When you have questions, contact your network administrator or help desk.

THE RECYCLE BIN

When you delete files in Windows 95, they are not immediately erased from the disk. They are moved to the Recycle Bin. To recover an accidentally deleted file, double-click on the Recycle Bin icon and choose the item or items you wish to restore. Then choose Restore from the File menu in the Recycle Bin window (see Figure B.3).

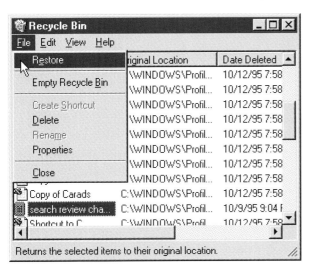

Figure B.3 The Recycle Bin gives you one more chance to "undelete" your files after trashing them

As you add new files to the Recycle Bin, Windows will eventually start discarding the earliest files left. If you want to free up space, right-click on the Recycle Bin and choose Empty Recycle Bin on the File menu.

FOLDERS

You and Windows 95 can organize your files into *folders,* which are the equivalent of directories in oldspeak. You can place folders within folders, thereby creating what used to be called subdirectories. You can create a new folder at any point by right-clicking on the desktop or in a folder (or disk drive) window and choosing New | Folder. You can put a document or program in a folder by dragging its icon onto a folder icon or into an open folder window.

NEW RULES FOR FILENAMES

Windows 95 allows you to use long filenames (up to 255 characters) that include spaces, if you want, so you can give your documents natural sounding names, instead of the pinched, cryptic filenames that DOS used to force on you. Now you can call that document *Amortization Projections for 1997* instead of AMTPRJ97.

You might also notice that filename extensions seem to have pretty much disappeared. They're still there at the ends of filenames, but Windows hides all the extensions it recognizes. If you want to see the extensions associated with all filenames, choose Options from the View menu in the My Computer window, the Windows Explorer window, or any folder (or disk drive) window. Click on the View tab. Then uncheck Hide MS-DOS file extensions for file types that are registered. Click on OK. All extensions will appear. To hide most extensions again, repeat the same steps and check the box.

When you are sharing files with non-Windows 95 users, and with programs that were sold prior to the release of Windows 95, filenames get shortened automatically. This can cause some confusion. Again, consult online help and Windows 95 books for details.

WINDOWS EXPLORER

Windows 95 allows you to look through the folders on your computer in a single window, with the entire folder tree in a pane on the left side (sort of like the old File Manager). To do this, choose Programs from the Start menu and Windows Explorer from the Programs menu (or right-click on any folder and choose Explore from the menu that pops up). The Windows Explorer window will appear (see Figure B.4), with its folder tree in the left pane and the contents of the selected folder in the right pane.

To see the contents of a folder, click on it in the left pane. To expand or collapse a folder's contents, double-click on the folder in the left pane (or click the little plus or minus icon in a box to the left of the folder). You can go up a folder level by pressing Backspace, as you can in any such window.

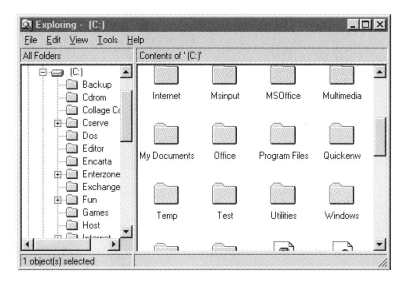

Figure B.4 The Explorer window shows a hierarchical view of the computer in its left pane. There you can thumb through your tree of folders without having to plow through separate folder windows

SHORTCUT ICONS

Windows 95 allows you to create *shortcut icons* that "point to" a program, document, folder, or other Windows 95 resource that you use regularly. This is particularly useful when something you use every day is "buried" in a folder within a folder. A popular place to keep shortcuts is on the desktop. That way, when you want to open your favorite folder, you just double-click on the shortcut icon on the desktop. Another place you can create a shortcut is on the Start menu, where it will look like a normal menu choice, not like a shortcut icon.

In general, the easiest way to create a shortcut is to right-click and drag a copy of the program's icon to the place where you want the shortcut. To do this, open the window that contains the program's original icon. Right-click on the icon and drag to a new location, such as another folder or the desktop. When you release the mouse button, a menu will pop up. Choose Create Shortcut(s) Here to make the shortcut. You'll probably want to rename the new shortcut icon. (Press F2, type a new name, and press ENTER.) If you drag an icon onto the Start button, even without first *right*-clicking, a shortcut to that icon will be placed on the Start menu.

THAT'S THE SHORT COURSE

Well, there you have a taste of Windows 95. Obviously, there's a lot more worth knowing. And the more you learn, the more productive you will become, so I encourage you to do some independent study, either by using Windows 95's online help or by cracking a good book or two.

Index

G

H

I

The Books to Use When There's No Time to Lose

Computer Fundamentals for Complicated Lives

Whether you set aside an *evening*, a *lunch hour*, or reach for a **Busy People** guide as you need it, you're guaranteed to save time with Windows 95 and its associated productivity applications. Organized for a quick orientation to Windows 95, Word, Excel, Access, and the Internet, each **Busy People** title offers exceptional time-saving features and has the right blend of vital skills and handy shortcuts that you must know to get a job done quickly and accurately. Full-color text make the going easy and fun.

Written by a busy person (like you!) with a skeptic's view of computing, these opinionated, well-organized, and authoritative books are all you'll need to master the important ins and outs of Windows 95 and other best-selling software releases—without wasting your precious hours!

Windows 95 for Busy People
by Ron Mansfield
$22.95 USA
ISBN: 0-07-882110-X
Available Now

Word for Windows 95 for Busy People
by Christian Crumlish
$22.95 USA
ISBN: 0-07-882109-6
Available Now

Excel for Windows 95 for Busy People
by Ron Mansfield
$22.95 USA
ISBN: 0-07-882111-8
Available Now

The Internet for Busy People
by Christian Crumlish
$22.95 USA
ISBN: 0-07-882108-8
Available Now

Access for Windows 95 for Busy People
by Alan Neibauer
$22.95 USA
ISBN: 0-07-882112-6
Available Now

To Order, Call Toll Free 1-800-822-8158

OSBORNE

Leaders of the Pack

The Internet Science, Research & Technology Yellow Pages
by Rick Stout and Morgan Davis
$22.95 U.S.A.
ISBN: 0-07-882187-8

The Internet Health, Fitness & Medicine Yellow Pages
by Matthew Naythons, M.D. with Anthony Catsimatides
$22.95 U.S.A.
ISBN: 0-07-882188-6

The Internet Yellow Pages Third Edition
by Harley Hahn
$29.95 U.S.A.
ISBN: 0-07-882182-7

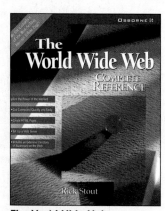

The World Wide Web Complete Reference
by Rick Stout
$29.95 U.S.A.
ISBN: 0-07-882142-8

NetLaw: Your Rights in the Online World
by Lance Rose
$19.95 U.S.A.
ISBN: 0-07-882077-4

The Internet Complete Reference Second Edition
by Harley Hahn
$32.95 U.S.A.
ISBN: 0-07-882138-X

   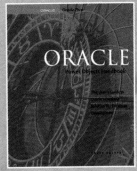